LESBIAN LOVE ADDICTION

LESBIAN LOVE ADDICTION

Understanding the Urge to Merge and How to Heal When Things Go Wrong

Lauren D. Cosine

ROWMAN & LITTLEFIELD
Lanham • Boulder • New York • London

Published by Rowman & Littlefield
A wholly owned subsidiary of The Rowman & Littlefield Publishing Group,
Inc.
4501 Forbes Boulevard, Suite 200, Lanham, Maryland 20706
www.rowman.com

Unit A, Whitacre Mews, 26-34 Stannary Street, London SE11 4AB

British Library Cataloguing in Publication Information Available

Library of Congress Cataloging-in-Publication Data

Costine, Lauren D.
Lesbian love addiction : Understanding the urge to merge and how to heal when things go wrong / by Lauren D. Costine.
pages cm.
Includes bibliographical references and index.
ISBN 978-1-4422-4808-3 (cloth : alk. paper) -- ISBN 978-1-4422-4809-0 (electronic)
1. Lesbians--Psychology. 2. Lesbians--Sexual behavior. 3. Relationship addiction. 4. Interpersonal relations. I. Title.
HQ75.5.C67 2015
306.76'63--dc23
2016019911

♾ ™ The paper used in this publication meets the minimum requirements of American National Standard for Information Sciences Permanence of Paper for Printed Library Materials, ANSI/NISO Z39.48-1992.

Printed in the United States of America

CONTENTS

Foreword   vii
Robert Weiss, LCSW, CSAT-S, Author, Clinician, Educator

Acknowledgments   xi

Introduction: Once Upon a Love Addiction   xiii

1   The Power of Our Physiology   1

2   The Way We Connect   17

3   What Is Unique about Lesbian Love Addiction?   37

4   How We Merge and Spiral   59

5   Withdrawal: What It is and How It Benefits Us   89

6   How to Have a Healthy Relationship with Yourself and Others   115

Notes   139

Index   149

About the Author   157

FOREWORD

Robert Weiss, LCSW, CSAT-S, Author, Clinician, Educator

The desire for intimate connection is at the core of human existence, and when we achieve meaningful bonds in form (our community, in romance, with family, friends, and community), it is fulfilling and magnificent to behold. Undeniably, our deep bonds with others are part of what makes life worthwhile. Sadly, however, due to traumatic early-life experiences, there are those who tend to abuse love, using the search for and experience of it to avoid being alone, or worse, as a self-centered source of stability and self-completion. These are people we consider to be love and sex "addicts," individuals who use love and sex to make themselves feel whole. For love and sex addicts, the experience of becoming known and knowing, of understanding and being understood, of acceptance and being accepted is not a mutual one. For such people, the healthy human need for connection is replaced by an endless, obsessive, and dysfunctional search for someone who will provide the kind of validation and self-worth that ultimately can only come from within ourselves.

These men and women become preoccupied (some to the point of obsession) with the idea of *falling in love* and *being in love* with someone and are less interested in a healthy engagement of shared interests, values, beliefs, and passions. Ultimately, what many love addicts are seeking is a lover/mother who will take care of them. This dysfunctional search for someone else who will *complete* them leads to related life problems such as anxiety, depression, low self-esteem, broken promises, abusive relationships, serial monogamy, sexual acting out, problems at work or in school, financial issues, poor self-care, and a diminished capacity to fully invest in their own lives.

In truth, love addicts are not chasing love. Instead, they are continually seeking the emotional intensity of early romance, or what is technically known as *limerence*, a phenomenon that Dr. Lauren Costine refers to as the "urge to merge." Essentially, limerence is the initial stage of a romantic relationship, when infatuation reigns and everything about the other person seems fabulous and perfect. The stuff that might drive a wedge between you later on—she feeds your cat table scraps, she spontaneously rearranges your closet, she spends too much time working—is completely overlooked. During limerence, when the urge to merge kicks in full force, potential relationship problems seem to not matter; they are simply a backseat to romantic intensity and excitement—for as long as those last.

Nearly everyone, addicted or not, has experienced the sensation of limerence, starting with their first schoolyard crush and moving on through pretty much every romantic relationship (or infatuation) that they've ever had, because it is part of the healthy human bonding experience. However, the vast majority of people are not love addicted, and they instinctively understand that healthy romantic connections are bonds that evolve over time from early intensity (limerence) to deeper, mutual interest and understanding (intimacy). In other words, people who are not love addicted inherently know that the powerful urge to merge is a temporary state, one that may or may not lead to long-lasting connection. Both male and female love addicts seek romantic intensity and use that experience of limerance—and all the drama that can go with it—to "get high" for the same reasons that sex addicts chase meaningless sexual engagements, that alcoholics drink, and drug addicts use.

For the most part, the dynamics of love addiction are the same regardless of gender or sexual orientation. For a diagnosis, three main elements must be present:

1. Preoccupation to the point of obsession with romantic relationships and activities
2. A loss of control over romantic relationships and activities (usually evidenced by failed attempts to quit or at least to cut back)

3. Negative consequences related to this out-of-control romantic pattern

People vulnerable to love addiction tend to be susceptible to other addictions as well as to emotional, psychological, and behavioral challenges related to early-life trauma and a genetic predisposition to addictive behavior. We find this to be true regardless of gender, race, culture, class, gender identity, or sexual orientation.

There are distinct differences between love addiction in women and men, and between heterosexuals and homosexuals. I first started discussing these important variations in the mid-1990s in papers and talks that primarily focused on the differences between straight male versus gay male sex addicts. This work led me to write *Cruise Control: Understanding Sex Addiction in Gay Men* in 2005. I felt rather strongly that both gay male sex addicts and the professionals who treat them needed to fully understand the world of gay male sexuality and lifestyle if they were ever going to adequately address pathological sexual behavior in gay men. Even in 2005, when I conceived the first edition of *Cruise Control* and related sex addiction in gay men to HIV/AIDS, my work was controversial, despite the fact that gay men were dying on a daily basis due to the undiagnosed and unrecognized problem of sexual addiction.

Soon after my initial publications and related lectures and clinical education on the topic, many of my peers and colleagues expressed apprehension about openly discussing gay sexual issues, fearing that any sort of public discourse on "gay sex addiction" would reinforce preexisting social homophobia. Others were angry and misrepresented this work as being "sex negative" and "sexually conservative," which could not be further from the truth. I continue to feel now, as I felt then: the fear of backlash is no reason to bury one's head in the sand and leave a needful treatment population underserved, while knowing fully that a "good looking family or community," which is unwilling to openly address their own problems, is doomed to stay stuck in them.

Happily, that was then and this is now. Today, *Cruise Control* is currently in its second edition and is now considered a staple of recovery by male sex addicts worldwide. As our culture has evolved and become more accepting of gay and lesbian individuals, people tend to thank rather than chide me for having written it. I am grateful to those who have written me over the years to say thank you.

Since I wrote the first edition of *Cruise Control* more than a decade ago, and revised it in 2013, I've felt strongly that a lesbian equivalent was needed. A few authors have chosen to address female sex and love addiction, in particular Kelly McDaniel with *Ready to Heal: Women Facing Love, Sex and Relationship Addiction* (2009) and Charlotte Kasl with *Women, Sex, and Addiction: A Search for Love and Power* (1998), however, no one has written specifically with a lesbian audience in mind. Those in need had to read heterosexually biased books and use a "gay filter," as gay people are often forced to do. Sadly, when it comes to self-help books, gay and lesbian readers have to sift through information designed for a heterosexual audience to interpret their own cultural experience.

Enter Dr. Lauren Costine with this excellent volume, written by and for the lesbian who deals with love addiction. I cannot imagine a more knowledgeable or empathetic professional woman to guide lesbian love addicts (along with their therapists and loved ones) through the often incomprehensible morass of active love addiction, recovery, and long-term healing. I met Lauren early in her psychotherapeutic career and immediately sensed her empathic interest and clinical talent. I've known her for several years now and am continually more impressed with her work over time. I am certain that this impassioned, engaged, thoughtful, and long-overdue book about the intricacies of identifying and recovering from love addiction will help countless lesbian and bisexual women. On a personal and professional level, I am so very grateful to Dr. Costine for having written it, not only because she has done so using examples and terminology which lesbian women will easily relate to and identify with, but also because her book offers clarity, direction, and hope to many women who didn't know there was hope to be found. As human beings who thrive in connection and wither in isolation, we all need and deserve the genuine and meaningful love that is possible to have with others, and with ourselves. This book surely forges a path toward realizing that.

ACKNOWLEDGMENTS

When it comes to writing a book there are never enough ways to thank all of the people who were behind its birth. This book is no exception. Its inception began years before any words were literally put on paper, but needless to say I am beyond grateful for the myriad of reasons this book exists today. First and foremost, I want to thank my clients and fellows in SLAA who allowed me to use parts of their stories to create the fictional characters you'll read about here. Without them this book would not have been possible. I want to thank my literary agent, Dana Newman, for believing in my book idea and procuring my first ever book deal with Rowan & Littlefield. I want to thank all the wonderful folks at Rowan & Littlefield for their invaluable help in making this book happen. I want to acknowledge my acquisitions and supervising editor, Suzanne Staszak-Silva, for taking a chance on me and for all her patience during my writing process. Thank you to Elaine McGarraugh, my production editor, for hanging in there through thick and thin. I want to thank Rob Weiss, who brought the need for such a book to my attention several years back and whose support through this entire process has been invaluable, to Brad Lamm for all of his support, and to all the LGBT activists and writers who have paved the way for books like this to even be possible today. To my lesbian-affirmative mentor Sandra Golvin, may she rest in peace, who helped me understand what it meant to be proud of my lesbian identity. I want to thank my mother, who struggled deeply with my lesbianism but who loved me through all of our misunderstandings and whom I loved madly and I

want to thank my father who has always been there for me and to whom
I also love madly. I want to thank my girlfriend, Vanessa, whose love
and support helped me stay sane during the roughest parts of meeting
my deadlines and all my friends, in recovery and out who have stuck by
my side through my own recovery from lesbian love addiction. All the
support and love I have received over the years from everyone who is a
major part of my life—I thank you.

INTRODUCTION

Once Upon a Love Addiction

It was a warm summer night in July, and Mary, an attractive, intelligent femme brunette, decided to join her usual group of lesbian pals at a lively, chic restaurant in Los Angeles. Whenever Mary went out she hoped she'd meet someone new, but that night she was not feeling particularly desperate. Then it happened. Standing at the bar, chatting with a friend and sipping her mocktail, Mary spotted a sexy brunette out of the corner of her eye. She felt immediately drawn to this woman who was just Mary's type—a soft butch with a Rachel Maddow look, short hair, and a tall, slender build. Mary was immediately turned on by her expressive eyes and creative, androgynous style. Promptly ending the conversation with her friend, Mary walked over and introduced herself to the woman. Her name was Jane.

Mary and Jane ended up deep in conversation for the rest of the night, talking passionately about life, love, and work, unaware of the other women around them. Mary found Jane's sense of humor and subtly sexy demeanor intriguing and her openness compelling. There were other things she couldn't quite put her finger on—just "something about Jane." There was one problem though: Jane had a girlfriend. "Damn," Mary thought, "don't the cute ones always have girlfriends?"

Little did Mary realize the night she met Jane that she would soon plunge into a deep well of love addiction, and only later discover just how profoundly it affected her life. It would take years to understand how to manage this addiction and prevent it from consuming her.

MARY'S RELATIONSHIP TO LOVE ADDICTION

Mary had already wrestled with alcohol and drugs earlier in her life. Thankfully, she was sober, and her life had gotten much better. Once she was in recovery, her career as an advertising executive took off.

Allowing herself to explore her true lesbian nature was also a big deal for Mary. Coming out to herself, her friends, and her family had not been easy. Her family's heterocentric (having a heterosexual bias and viewing heterosexuality as superior to any other sexual orientation) values and, in particular, her mother's negative feelings about same-sex love, deeply affected her.[1] Mary was in her late twenties before she finally embraced her attraction to women and freely discussed her sexuality. Once Mary overcame her struggles with coming out, she immersed herself in the lesbian community, giving her a sense of pride and security. Her career took off, and she started living her life to the fullest. Coming out had unleashed an excitement around sex and love that Mary hadn't experienced before, and with these new feelings she jumped into multiple and often overlapping romantic and sexual experiences.

After discovering Jane wasn't available, Mary decided not to pursue her. Not that night, anyway. But she didn't forget about her. Over the next couple of years, Mary would run into Jane at various lesbian functions. Every now and then she would find herself fantasizing about Jane and the possibility of a relationship, imagining that something very special existed between them. On one occasion she woke up with a start, breathless from the explicit sexual dream she'd had about the two of them. Thinking of Jane in these sexual and romantic ways made her ultra-excited and triggered a sense of aliveness she did not experience any other way. She loved—*loved!*—being this attracted to another woman and was enthralled by the idea that she was even capable of such a special connection. These reflections made her feel good about herself. She would feel varying degrees of euphoria exploring this fantasy life. She felt wonderful and full of hope.

In those moments, those fleeting seconds, Mary felt free of all the mundane and frustrating aspects of her life. Feeling this high made life seem exhilarating and worth living. It softened the shame she had carried around with her since she was a child. It diminished daily hardships and challenges; extinguished her feelings of loneliness, unworthiness, and self-hatred; and muted the voices in her head that told her she wasn't good enough or deserving of a great life. In those very precious moments, all the problems, resentments, and difficulties she struggled with vanished.

WHAT IS LOVE ADDICTION?

At this point in human evolution, most of us are familiar with addiction and the effect it can have on everyone, including the friends and family members of the addict. The effects of alcohol and drug abuse, which can be life threatening and lead to violent acts, are fairly obvious. Sex addiction came out of the closet more recently and has been prominently exposed in the media. However, the focus has mainly been on heterosexual men. Sex addiction has been the subject of a number of movies including *Shame*, *Don Jon*, and *Thanks for Sharing*, all of which have highlighted straight male sex addicts, and the damage it does to the men and their loved ones.[2] The 2012 romantic comedy *Thanks for Sharing* is the story of several sex addicts and the twelve-step recovery program they use to overcome their addiction. The movie is funny and warm while still educating its audience on the seriousness of the topic— that sex addiction destroys lives, but one can recover when motivated and be willing to do what it takes to get better, such as going to a twelve-step program.[3]

HOW IS LOVE ADDICTION DIFFERENT FROM SEX ADDICTION?

While sex and love addiction may overlap in some people, for others the two can be quite separate. Both involve getting high from their respective drugs: sex or love. But sex addicts get high solely through acts that are compulsive and involve sex such as daily or weekly anonymous sex, hiring prostitutes, porn, and masturbation.[4] Love addicts get their high by falling in love, obsessing about another person, never being alone, serial monogamy, or the fantasy of falling in love with or having a relationship with other people.[5] Sometimes it involves sex with the desired person, but sometimes it does not.

While many helpful books have been written on love addiction for women, most are heterosexually focused, which leaves women who love women—whether they identify as lesbian, bisexual, queer, fluid, or pansexual—with little understanding of how love addiction can affect them. Love addiction has serious consequences for women with varying styles of LGBTQ identity, including lesbian, bi, fluid (having a more fluctuating sense of sexuality that includes attraction to any gender), queer (an identity that embraces all same-sex love, gender identities, and gender expressions as their own—they feel connected to every identity within the spectrum of the LGBTQ community), or pansexual (an identity that encompasses an attraction to all people). These women suffer greatly from many of the destructive and often unconscious behaviors and emotional demands that this addiction creates.[6]

Since the 1980s to the present day, several love addiction pioneers and twelve-step programs have defined love addiction in various ways. The characteristics used to help organize the definition for this book are from Pia Mellody's *Facing Love Addiction*, Sex and Love Addicts Anonymous' (SLAA) literature, and Anne Wilson Schaef's *Escape from Intimacy*. Each of these books have been invaluable in helping me sort through the myriad of available explanations. The lesbian psyche was kept in mind the entire time this was thought out. If you think that love addiction might be a problem in your life, ask yourself if you possess any of these characteristics.

Characteristics of a Love Addict

1. A love addict idealizes the woman she falls in love with and often assigns magical qualities to her. Love addicts become preoccupied with the idealized woman and spend an inordinate amount of time thinking about her and longing to be with her. This "falling in love" process creates a physical high as the brain releases dopamine and oxytocin when they are sexually and romantically

attracted to another women. These "feel good" chemicals are potent for most lesbians, and for the addict they can be addictive.

2. Love addicts have difficulty setting boundaries and holding on to their individual identities. They tend to trust too quickly and become vulnerable without maintaining healthy boundaries. Lesbian love addicts pursue and get deeply involved with women before knowing enough about who their potential mate is and if there is any potential for compatibility.

3. Love addicts have unrealistic expectations for a relationship and need constant "unconditional positive regard" from their partners. Due to their attachment issues and childhood and societal trauma, they suffer greatly when their unrealistic need is not met and the high of falling in love is threatened.

4. A love addict will stop caring for herself in the relationship—emotionally, physically, or financially—and neglect friends and family. She will value pleasing her partner at all costs, compromising her own sense of self.

5. Because they secretly feel unlovable, love addicts use love, relationships, sex, and romance to stave off feelings of unworthiness, emptiness, loneliness, sadness, grief, anger, guilt, and shame.

6. Unable to tolerate being alone, some women will jump from relationship to relationship, taking no responsibility for why the last one didn't work and pursuing the high of a new romantic love at all costs.[7]

MARY'S ADDICTION INCREASES OVER TIME

Over the years, Mary and Jane ran into each other at various events. One such event was an afternoon lesbian gathering in the spring of 2013, about two years after they met. It was a beautiful sunny day, and the party was made up of women in good moods socializing. The food was delicious, and the vibe enticing. Mary arrived with her current girlfriend, Tina, whom she loved deeply, but when she saw Jane across the yard her heart stopped. Again, she felt that exhilarating jolt, that thrilling feeling of being alive. "Wow," she thought, "Jane looks hot." Since Jane was also with another woman, they said "hi" to each other and moved on, but Mary couldn't ignore the energy she immediately felt in Jane's presence.

Over the next few months, Jane and Mary connected on Facebook and Instagram, where Mary would occasionally find herself following Jane's activities to see what she was doing. Whenever she ran into Jane, Mary would experience that raw, animal-like attraction all over again— her heart would race, her palms would get sweaty, and that rush would return. Mary was fairly confident that Jane shared these feelings, but much as she desired a relationship with Jane, one of them always seemed to be in a relationship with another woman. The timing was never right.

MARY IS NEVER ALONE FOR LONG

Like many love addicts, Mary was never single for very long, if at all. If she wasn't in a relationship, she was chasing after the promise of a new one. Being in a relationship addressed Mary's normal, healthy needs— feeling safe, loved, and secure in the world—but it also fed Mary's love addiction. Being chased by women made her feel attractive, desirable, and powerful. Not all of her relationships had the same level of sexual and romantic stimulation, but each meant something very special.

Such was the case with Tina, a charming, soft butch with short auburn hair, a contagious smile, and a big heart. Unfortunately for Mary, Tina struggled with sobriety and love addiction. Though each of them often claimed to be the love of each other's life, Tina's feelings toward Mary would fluctuate, and when the heat waned she would become emotionally avoidant, distancing herself until she was emotionally gone from the relationship, or leave it all together. Their connection was intense, but it constantly cycled in and out. The two were always hot or cold, getting together or breaking up. In fact, it was during this on-again, off-again eight-year pattern with Tina that Mary met Jane. Each time she pursued Mary, Tina would express her undying love and promise that things would be different this time and that she had changed and finally gotten sober, and the two would reconcile. "Please," she would vow, "give me the chance to prove how much I love you. I'll be different this time, I promise."

Each reunion was deeply complicated for both women. The process of reconciling was exciting and fulfilling, and the high of those honeymoons became a compulsion and a big part of the addiction. Inevitably a breakdown in communication and connection would take place, and once again Tina would change her mind and call it quits, declaring yet again that she "just couldn't do this."

When this pattern first emerged, Mary was devastated. She'd find herself on the floor, curled up in a ball, sobbing uncontrollably, or walking around in a stupor, barely able to eat. In the early stages of their addictive cycling, Mary was not yet out to her parents, so she had to hide her pain from them and pretend she was fine. Mary found the rock of support she needed in a therapist, and she eventually recovered from the shock of losing someone she thought she would spend the rest of her life with. This was the first time anyone had affected her this deeply, and though Mary had some understanding of what this trauma was eliciting inside of her, she was not yet sober, and so, like many addicts, she turned to alcohol and drugs to help her deal with these overwhelming feelings.

Because Tina was always the one coming and going, breaking up, then wanting out, Mary didn't feel much responsibility for this pattern. She considered this Tina's issue. With time and the help of a therapist, Mary became more aware of how toxic the cycles with Tina were and started to feel embarrassed by them. She sensed something profoundly dysfunctional and painful about their relationship, but she was not yet aware that her addiction to Tina's unpredictable declarations and drama was part of the problem. She did, however, recognize its craziness and knew it was unsustainable, and this realization led her to seek out answers. Chief among those was learning that Tina was *love avoidant*.

LOVE AVOIDANTS

Pia Mellody's groundbreaking research on love avoidants is well described in *Facing Love Addiction*, which lays out the characteristics, many unconscious, of the love avoidant—a term a friend of her coined during their research on love addiction.[8] It is also well described by Amir Levine and Rachel Heller in their book, *Attached: The New Science of Adult Attachment and How It Can Help You Find—and*

Keep—Love. We'll look at love avoidants more closely in chapter 2, but the following is a short summary of love avoidant behaviors:

Love Avoidant Behaviors

1. Fear of authentic and lasting intimacy within a relationship, leading to emotional distancing and unavailability.
2. Fear of being truly known by the other person, which could bring up intolerable feelings of shame, unworthiness, and unlovability.
3. Fear of being smothered by a partner, which leads to avoiding most intimate contact once the chase and honeymoon periods are over.
4. Blaming and finding fault with a partner to maintain distance, emotionally and sexually.
5. Criticizing and belittling the partner to push her away and avoid feeling smothered.[9]

Unfortunately, love addicts and love avoidants are often drawn to each other and end up together. In the love addiction dynamic, the first flush of a relationship is awash in euphoria, at least until the love addict's need for constant love, sex, gratification, and unconditional positive regard is no longer met. The love avoidant, who may exhibit love addict behavior in the beginning, will start pulling away once her intimacy issues are triggered and the need to push her partner away is activated. As the love avoidant begins to pull away emotionally, psychologically, and sexually, the love addict, being finely attuned to subtle alterations in their connection, senses the love avoidant's change in behavior. This cycle prompts a desperate need to recreate the honeymoon period with her partner and launches both women into falling further and further into dysfunctional and painful coping styles. At this time, hopelessness usually sets in for both women.

MARY'S ATTACHMENT PATTERNS REVEALED

Today's research on relationships, which includes studies on attachment theory, communication patterns, and love addiction, has revised our understanding of the human need for love and emotional connection.

In the 1950s, psychologists John Bowlby and Mary Ainsworth studied the relationship between mothers and their infants. Decades of their empirical data have allowed relationship experts to understand and thus address people's needs more effectively. This change in the relationship landscape has led to books (like this one) that can help those struggling with destructive relationship patterns in ways previously unimagined. We will explore each modality in more depth, but for now let's look at attachment theory to help us understand more about Mary's situation.

ATTACHMENT THEORY

Attachment theory gives us invaluable information about our adult relationship patterns, which relate to how we were cared for as infants. Bowlby and Ainsworth's goal was to understand how the infant–primary caretaker relationship might affect a child's psychological development.[10] What they found revolutionized what we know today about natural relationships and our attachment needs.

After decades of research that amplifies the work of Bowlby and Ainsworth, we now know that the central nervous system is wired for connection.[11] As humans, we seek out and require close, reliable, trustworthy relationships for our very survival. This need was present when humans were first developing hundreds of thousands of years ago. To survive, a baby needed a caretaker (usually the mother) he or she could trust completely. As human adults, we form attachments with a select few for protection. These relationships are necessary, providing a way for us to watch out for each other in a dangerous world.

These attachment patterns that were imprinted onto our early ancestors, and later our caretakers, follow us into our sexual relationships. Our need for secure relationships is hardwired into our central nervous system, and any interruption in a significant relationship, especially during our first pivotal relationships, can injure our central nervous system. If, for example, a toddler who is attached to her mother or primary caretaker is taken away from him or her, she will experience a physiological wound. As Levine and Heller state in their book *Attached*, when a separation occurs with someone to whom you are deeply attached, the body experiences it physically, in the same way one might experience a broken leg.[12] That is why losing someone you deeply love is physiologically—emotionally and physically—painful.

From this perspective, we can see that Mary is acting from an innate desire for love and security. Her natural desire for a loving and secure partner is hardwired into her entire physiological (central nervous) and psychological (psyche) system. Mary's desire to make the relationship work with Tina, someone she is deeply attached to, is natural. Her inability to leave Tina, even after years of being emotionally abandoned by her, shows that something may have gone terribly wrong during Mary's early attachment years. We will explore this in greater detail in chapter 3, but for Mary, and for all lesbians, her relationship with her mother created a blueprint for later relationship choices. The problems with her mother, one of her core life relationships, created pain she continues to carry with her. This pain, combined with her addiction, led Mary to the destructive patterns of love addiction so evident in her life.

MARY'S MULTIPLE RELATIONSHIPS

During one of her numerous breakups with Tina, Mary met Sophia and started to date her exclusively. Sophia was a femme whom Mary felt immediately drawn to, and whose grounded, down-to-earth nature was a comfort to Mary and made her feel safe. Unlike Mary's typical choices, Sophia was not overly seductive or flirtatious. She could delve into a deep conversation without much pretext. Although Sophia was more femme physically than Mary was typically drawn to, Mary knew Sophia would be loyal and true to her word—something she craved after Tina's emotional tug of war. Their honeymoon period was lovely, and Mary was hopeful that this relationship could last. In the initial stages, they bought gifts for each other, talked every day, met each other's family, and settled into a committed, loving relationship just weeks after their first date.

Initially, Mary found their relationship fulfilling because she always felt better and safer when she was in a relationship, despite any possible tumult and drama. Over time, however, Mary's love addiction emerged. Obsessed with looking at beautiful women and talking about it to whomever would listen, Mary would point out women she found "hot" to Sophia, who was not at all enticed by these conversations. On the contrary, the comments made Sophia feel insecure. Because Sophia wasn't showing her true feelings, she reacted with anger whenever Mary noticed other women, which made Mary feel smothered. Jealousy became a big problem in their relationship, and Mary found herself pulling away emotionally and sexually as her own love-avoidant issues emerged. Unable to be accountable for her own part in the dynamic, she grew to resent Sophia's jealousy and insecure behavior, pulling further and further away, until she eventually lost her desire to have sex or be intimate.

And then, something not altogether surprising occurred. Remember, Mary had just left a relationship that included an untrustworthy partner and many heartbreaks. As a reaction to her own dissatisfaction and Sophia's jealousy and angry outbursts, Mary started *intriguing*— engaging in flirtatious, usually inappropriate behaviors—to avoid her own intimacy issues and create that feeling of aliveness she craved. Can you guess who Mary focused her intriguing on during her relationship with Sophia? If you guessed Tina, you are correct.

Mary loved Sophia, but she grew weary of their day-to-day problems and became bored once the initial excitement subsided. As she engaged with Tina, Mary rationalized that the special connection she had with Tina drew them together, when in reality it was her addiction to intrigue and the hit of falling in love that lured her back in. So when Tina came along with that honeymoon-like intensity, Mary started seeing Tina behind Sophia's back. Eventually this led to an emotionally painful breakup, leaving Mary extremely guilt ridden, but unable to stop. She dreamed that Tina's promise of love and excitement would be permanent this time, and thus save her.

It did not take much for Tina to convince Mary that this time would be different, and soon after they started communicating again the bottom dropped out. Right when Mary cut things off with Sophia, Tina informed her she was seeing someone else, someone she was getting serious with—a detail Tina had neglected to share with Mary while they were intriguing. As annoyed and hurt as Mary was, she continued to believe that the history she shared with Tina would trump the feelings she might have for the new woman who came along.

Another pattern Mary had developed during her relationships was withdrawing from her friends. Now that she and Sophia were over, Mary was enjoying her freedom and reaching out to her friends again.

Though she missed the special connection she had with Sophia, she was relieved to be away from their daily conflicts and waning sex life. Meanwhile, Mary and Tina continued to see each other (and text each other) without Tina's new girlfriend's knowledge, on the pretext that they were just friends.

Seated near the beautiful gardens of the Getty Museum one afternoon, Tina and Mary sat close, unable to ignore the chemistry between them, or keep themselves from touching the other. It was exciting to flirt and watch the beautiful orange and magenta sunset together, and Tina must have recognized what Mary was communicating with her eyes: *I want you so badly. I would tear off your clothes right now if I could—that's how hot this moment is.* However much Tina held to her position that she was seeing someone new, she was also carefully leaving the door open for Mary, who found her mixed messages and the thrill of the chase intoxicating. What Mary experienced was literally a high, a hit of dopamine and oxytocin that her brain released physically while engaging with Tina. It was exhilarating.

Each encounter, each text, each phone call gave Mary that feeling of euphoria, that physical sensation that she was addicted to. Mary would leave each encounter feeling alive, fantasizing about their future together. The intrigue, the feeling that anything was possible, was like receiving another heavy injection of her drug. Other women pursued Mary, and she loved this kind of attention, but the highs weren't quite as enticing as those she got from her love avoidant Tina.

WHAT'S MERGING GOT TO DO WITH IT?

Merging is a major theme in many lesbian relationships, especially those that are riddled with love addiction. Since merging is such an important concept to this book, I want to give it undivided attention here.

The Urge to Merge

Merging is when two women who have an immediate, intense, intimate physical and emotional attraction to one another start spending all of their time together. Feeling so connected and close creates such pleasure that the urge to become almost one is too tempting to deny. Being unconscious to its downside, both women jump into the relationship without taking the time to get to know one another outside of any intense physical or emotional context.

The thrill of merging—from the honeymoon phase to the point at which lesbians find themselves in unhealthy relationships they don't know how to leave—is hard to resist. Merging is necessary and healthy in early relationships, especially during the bonding/attachment phase. But when love addiction is involved, in one or both of the women, merging takes on an unhealthy quality. For many women this means losing herself in the other woman, and watching her sense of self, which was fragile to begin with, become more unstable. Fear of abandonment starts to dictate the woman's unconscious and conscious thoughts.

Merging behaviors can start to develop in the early stages of the relationship and often follow this pattern:

1. Dating evolves immediately into a relationship.
2. The two spend every night at each other's house, or move in together too quickly.
3. Friendships are neglected and fall away.
4. Each woman becomes afraid to communicate her real feelings for fear of hurting or pushing her new love away.
5. A need to agree on everything develops. Differences of opinion get silenced, and opposing needs or desires are seen as threatening.
6. Jealousy of other women is heightened. Behind this is a deep insecurity of one's lovability, which morphs into a need to control the other's ability to leave.

Merging too quickly is unhealthy and harmful to each woman's fragile sense of self. It often leads to a painful or disastrous end of the relationship. Unfortunately, lesbians who suffer from love addiction often mistake merging, and the intensity that accompanies it, for love.

Merging and its relationship to love addiction is central to the concepts in this book. We will explore the origins, purpose, and consequences of merging, and the cancerous quality it has on relationships and on one's sense of self. The good news is that recognizing and treat-

ing love addiction can happen, and a fulfilling life and healthy relationships await those who commit to healing it.

WHAT'S NEXT?

Love addiction and love avoidance are still relatively new concepts, yet
popular songs about the highs of falling in love and the devastation that
occurs when love doesn't work out are everywhere, and many of them
exemplify love addiction narratives. There are many romantic films that
portray love addiction unconsciously, or promote the idea that love is a
perpetual honeymoon and that love will conquer all. In lesbian films,
we see women falling for unavailable women, inappropriate pairings,
being unfaithful, or jumping from one relationship to another. In both
films and popular television shows, love addiction is often portrayed as
the norm, and unattainable ideals and devastating heartbreak are de-
picted as inevitable in lesbian relationships. Films like *Loving Annabelle*, *High Art*, *My Summer of Love*, *Tipping the Velvet*, and television
shows such as *The L Word* and, ironically, the reality show, *The Real L
Word*, perpetuate stereotypes that paint lesbians as desperately seeking
love, and merging, at any cost,[13] and most importantly, the false belief
that merging works.

Thankfully, mental health experts are helping us move beyond these
unhealthy relationship and relational models. Dr. Patrick Carnes's
groundbreaking book, *Out of the Shadows: Understanding Sexual Addiction*, was the first book written about sex addiction in heterosexual
men. There are several important works on love and sex addiction in
heterosexual women, such as Robin Norwood's *Women Who Love Too
Much: When You Keep Wishing and Hoping He'll Change*; *Ready to
Heal* by Kelly McDaniel; and *Facing Love Addiction: Giving Yourself
the Power to Change the Way You Love* by Pia Mellody. In 2005,
Robert Weiss, founder of the Sexual Recovery Institute, wrote *Cruise
Control: Understanding Sex Addiction in Gay Men*, the only book on
gay male sex addiction to date. The success of Weiss's work and his
personal suggestions and guiding force helped inspire this book. Despite these extraordinary advances, there is still a lot of denial and
naivety about the destructive effects of love addiction on women. And

little is known or discussed about this phenomenon for lesbians, bisexual women, and all women who love women.

The reality, however, is that love addiction can also be a deadly addiction, though it isn't often assigned the same seriousness as, for example, a drug addiction. This is because love addiction is harder to see, and therefore, harder to treat. Thankfully, there are now treatment centers for love addiction, although they tend to be heterosexually oriented and less knowledgeable in their treatment approaches to the lesbian psyche. While lesbians can get love addiction help at these treatment centers, the unique issues faced by lesbians battling this addiction aren't likely to be addressed.

This book is written for lesbians, but it is also valuable for anyone interested in learning more about destructive and painful romantic patterns of love addiction. I pledge to help you find a way out, to do my best to explain what you are going through so that you can get the help you need and deserve. I have included a variety of love addiction stories throughout this book. My hope is that if you don't see your story here, you will at least find some of the questions and answers you are struggling with. The second half of the book provides tools on how to heal from this painful and destructive addiction.

1

THE POWER OF OUR PHYSIOLOGY

Girls love each other like animals. There is something ferocious and unself-conscious about it. . . . No one trains us to shield our hearts from each other. With girls, it's total vulnerability from the beginning. . . . And it's relentless.

—*Black Iris*, by Leah Raeder[1]

As we can see from the introduction, lesbian love addiction can have devastating life consequences. Lesbian love addiction is also complicated because love, in and of itself, is not a problem substance in the way that drugs or alcohol are for the addict or the alcoholic. The pain and misery that lesbian love addiction creates isn't a result of getting too much love. It is the desire for love at any cost, the all-consuming need for love, and the overreliance on your love interest to provide you with an overall sense of worth that gives it the addictive quality. However, overcoming and healing from lesbian love addiction does not require removing love from your life. Recovery isn't about avoiding relationships. The path to recovery involves learning how to build a healthy relationship. Studies show that finding love and learning how to create a loving, mutually respectful relationship can be an essential ingredient for a fulfilling life.[2]

Happiness is certainly one of the greatest benefits of a healthy romantic partnership, but to have that we must first create a compassionate and nourishing relationship with ourselves. Once we become aware of our compulsive need to be partnered and begin to understand what causes our addiction to love at any price, we're on our way to achieving that relationship. Let's start with what happens in our bodies.

All addictions have physical components, and love addiction is no exception. The physical components of love addiction have a biological component, originating in the body itself, via neuropathways in the brain. Therefore, we can learn a lot from looking at the physiological components of love and relationships for lesbians by examining the female brain. To do this, we start with one woman who made one of the biggest contributions to the field of neuropsychiatry.

THE FEMALE BRAIN

Dr. Louann Brizendine was a young medical student specializing in psychiatry in the late 1970s when she observed that much of medicine was based on studies done exclusively on the male brain. When Brizendine asked her professors at Harvard why the female brain was never used to collect data for medical use, she was told it was because women's menstrual cycles would skew the data. Unfortunately, this kind of oversight was part of the prevailing attitude of the male-focused medical establishment at the time. Thankfully, Brizendine focused her studies on looking at woman's brains and hormonal systems to see how they affect the way we think, feel, and act.

Recognizing this huge gap in medicine, Brizendine opened up her own clinic to conduct studies and collect and study data on the female brain and hormonal systems. By looking at every stage of the brain's development, from the female brain in prenatal studies to the unique qualities of the aging brain, her findings were nothing short of revolutionary.

Her work has led to great developments in our understanding of women in relationships from a biological perspective. In other words, this is a helpful way to understand our physiology. Our upbringing and parenting bring the nurturing part. This is often referred to in the psychology world as "nature versus nurture." One of this book's goals is to highlight how nature and nurture work in tandem when addictions develop. For this section we will study how our nature can play a part in lesbian love addiction.

Brizendine's 2006 book, *The Female Brain*,[3] is an in-depth exploration of the ways in which women's unique brain structure, hormones—in particular estrogen, progesterone, and testosterone—and neurotransmitters differentiate women's brains from men's. Controversial in some academic circles[4] because of its emphasis on gender differences and fixed brain patterns,[5] it nonetheless gives us information that is useful in understanding lesbian love addiction when applied in the correct context and with skepticism.[6]

According to Brizendine, over the last hundreds of thousands of years, our brains have developed in relation to our evolutionary needs and the survival of the species. A crucial factor in securing the continuation of species is the ability to seek connection and understand other people. Evolutionarily speaking, women have been the progenitors of this role, and the biological need to secure human connection has been imprinted on us. Through a complex set of neuronal pathways and hormonal systems, which change throughout the life cycle, the female brain is neurologically wired to find—and figure out how to sustain—meaningful relationships. Although some of this ingrained behavior may seem less relevant for women in the twenty-first century, it is important to remember that our brains deliver instructions based more on our thousands of years of programming, than our contemporary lifestyle avail us.

Gay Women

While Brizendine's book offers an important perspective and a deeper understanding of how women naturally operate in the world, its heterocentric interpretations of women's behavior are focused on the evolutionary responsibility of heterosexual mating. While this makes sense from a primal perspective and, of course, is true for many women, sensitivity to lesbian differences falls short in this analysis.

Furthermore, not all women choose to become mothers and have children as Brizendine's work would have us believe that the female brain is designed to do. Despite what appears to be an increase in lesbian couples having children, only 25 percent of lesbians in the United States have children.[7] Given the wide range of lesbian lifestyles and partnering choices, from single life to domestic partnerships and marriages, which may include being parents, Brizendine's study is limited in its application to women who love women. Despite these shortcomings, *The Female Brain* will prove helpful.

Could There Be a Lesbian Brain?

While many scientists are still busy looking for a gay gene, Brizendine provides an addendum in the back of the book with information about the gay women's brain and how it might compare to a heterosexual women's brain. However, the findings are sparse. Brizendine found that when a developing female is exposed to a higher level of testosterone in-utero, she will have more "typical" male brain characteristics such as tomboyish behaviors in childhood and less sensitive auditory and verbal fluency responses, traits more common in males. More recent research in the field of epigenetics indicates that some developing fetuses can be more sensitive to hormone exposure, a combination of their own adrenal gland production and the mother's endocrine system, while others are resistant to excess testosterone. The subject as it relates to gender and sexual orientation is controversial, as well as complicated by individual gene expression. However, Brizendine's findings indicate that female embryos exposed to higher levels of testosterone are more likely to produce offspring who later identify as lesbian, gay, bisexual, transgender, or queer (LGBTQ).

Dr. Norman Doidge offers us the opportunity to look at sexuality in another way. In his book, *The Brain That Changes Itself: Stories of Personal Triumph from the Frontiers of Brain Science*, he discusses how human sexuality defies the laws of evolutionary-based science. Doidge's work highlights human's tremendous variety when it comes to our sexuality. He states, "Human beings exhibit an extraordinary degree of sexual plasticity compared with other creatures,"[8] discussing how our attractions, desires, types, and even sexual orientations can change over one's lifetime.

Unfortunately, there is a lack of studies at this time on the lesbian brain that might explain the nuances of sexual orientation for femme-identified, butch-identified, or androgynous lesbians. I look forward to more in-depth studies being conducted in these areas. For now, let's focus on what we do know about the female brain and use some of Brizedine's and other brain researchers' findings to help us better understand lesbian behavior in relation to love addiction.

The Female Brain in Utero

This might come as a surprise to some, but in the first eight weeks of development, all fetuses are female. This means that in those two months our brains have already developed specific neuronal pathways that create, among other characteristics, our desire to be connected to other human beings. With its two X chromosomes, the female brain develops traits related to emotions, communication, and interpersonal interactions that can be considered female brain specific:

- Mirror neurons that help us interpret the actions of others and empathize (may also influence how we communicate)
- Gut feelings
- Emotional memory
- An ability to read people's emotions in nuanced ways
- Innate nurturing skills
- Hardwired to empathize
- Access to both sides of the brain easily
- Well-developed emotional control

Dr. Brizendine's research was the first of its kind to show that the female brain differs from the male brain as a result of hormonal changes. Contrary to previous medical and scientific belief systems, her work shows just how the female brain's configuration, relay centers, and neuronal pathways are positioned differently than those of the male brain. One of the key mechanisms of the female brain is its ability to relate, communicate, interpret, love, and nurture. Add to this a specific hormonal system geared toward communication and nurturing, and you can see that in our biological makeup, women are predispositioned to connect. This is only recently understood in a way that allows physicians and psychologists to help women understand themselves better.

This information also takes away the shame that the patriarchal, heterocentric ideology has placed on the way women not only relate to others but the process and disseminate information. By knowing that our brains are designed to function in a way that not only ensures human survival but is also based in emotional intelligence related to love and human connection elevates our unique role on the planet. This means that women play an intrinsic part in humanity's ability to become healthy, compassionate, nurturing individuals.

While this is a book about and for women who love women and our current understanding of gender is flawed, aspects of Brizendine's research that compares the male and female brain does help us see women's strengths in new and exciting ways. The female's and male's different brain sizes were kept in mind when comparing the different region's dimensions. Looking at these differences can also help when trying to comprehend what it means to live and thrive in a culture that has been predicated on male-centric ideals.

Testosterone

At eight weeks, the developing fetus that received a Y chromosome will begin to produce testosterone, which saturates the brain and creates male genitalia. During this period of gender assignment, the testosterone starts breaking down some of the connective tissues that the brain had originally. Interestingly, those connective tissues remain in the brains of females, and they are what orient women to be relationally focused.

THE FEMALE BRAIN STRUCTURES

Once developed, the female brain is composed of several components:

Prefrontal Cortex: This area of the brain helps us regulate our emotions and develop executive functioning skills. Decision making, impulse control, and planning all happen here. It is also where we access our wisdom and rational thoughts.

Amygdala: We hold our more "shadowy" feelings such as fear, anger, rage, shame, sadness, and aggression in the amygdala, which is regulated by the prefrontal cortex. This is the place in the psyche where we hide or repress negative emotions. This is smaller in women than men.

Hypothalamus: Also considered our hormonal relay center, the hypothalamus manages our hormones and activates our gonads in early adolescence. It regulates the automatic nervous system, which houses the sympathetic and parasympathetic nervous systems.

Pituitary Gland: This little gland has a big job. It produces our fertility and sexual hormones and turns on the nurturing brain when needed. It is what guides moms to start mothering and encourages women to care about others.

Hippocampus: This is our memory center, the area that stores those luscious romantic encounters, traumas, and painful betrayals. Women have a larger hippocampus than men do.

Anterior Cingulate Cortex: This is where the brain's worry center is located, and where we engage in critical thinking. The anterior cingulate cortex (ACC) is bigger in women than in men.

Insula: This area processes our intuition, those feelings inside of us that we often call our "gut feelings." It is also larger in women.

Limbic System

The limbic system is the area in the brain that holds our emotional and motivational center—the hypothalamus, hippocampus, and amygdala. The limbic system is connected to our need to survive. Interestingly, it is also linked to our pleasure center. Addictive tendencies and the often uncontrollable desire for pleasure originate here.[9]

Knowing more about how each area of the brain functions will give us a deeper understanding of how love addiction works. The natural connective tissues in the female brain instinctively point women in the direction of relationships, but they can also lead women to abuse the desire to connect. This can be especially true, as well as dangerous, for lesbians.

Central Nervous System

The central nervous system (CNS) is responsible for processing and interpreting all of the body's information via neurons. The main organs of this system are the brain and spinal cord, which are constantly interacting with one another through a special chemical system of neurotransmitters. The autonomic nervous system (ANS) rests inside the CNS.[10]

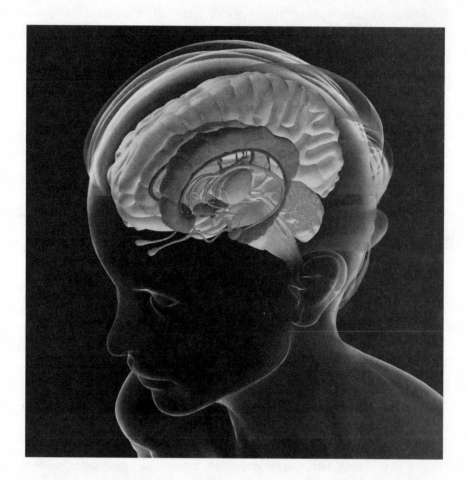

Figure 1.1. The Female Brain: thalamus (the long highlighted piece that curves around the top), amygdala (small bulb), and hippocampus (shady area under the amygdala), and hypothalamus (long dark curved piece under the thalamus). © Copyright 1999–2015 Getty Images

Autonomic Nervous System

The ANS is situated throughout the body and is connected to many regions in the body that work outside of our awareness, such as our heartbeat, digestion, and sexual organs. But its role is more far reaching than that. It is composed of two main parts: the sympathetic nervous system (SNS) and the parasympathetic nervous system (PNS).

Sympathetic Nervous System

This is the part of our ANS that gets us going. It helps get us out of bed in the morning to make that morning coffee, exercise, and get to work or school. It is most well known for being in charge of our fight-or-flight response. Through a complex system of neuronal pathways, cell activity, and hormonal communication, the SNS helps us accomplish our goals and make our dreams come true. Simply put, it is our excitatory system and therefore is connected to cortisol. It is also key to our emotional well-being. When it is working well, we feel motivated and energized. When it is out of balance, we have a harder time functioning effectively, which can affect our mood and our self-esteem.

Parasympathetic Nervous System

The PNS does the exact opposite job of the SNS. It tells us to relax and calm down when the day is over and we have accomplished what we needed to. It also aids in our digestion because it allows our bodies to rest while our digestive system goes to work, which is why it is sometimes referred to as "rest and digest" (and in a heterocentric context, "feed and breed"). We'll see how this all relates to the women's sex drive later, but for now it is important to understand its basic role, which is to calm us down so we can relax, rejuvenate, and experience pleasure.

Ideally, these two systems are working together to create balance in our bodies—and in our lives. If they are not working harmoniously as a result of trauma, stressful environments, or post-traumatic stress disorder (PTSD), the body and mind suffer. In this state, we need help from therapists, support groups, twelve-step programs, friends, or family members, which can help us bring balance back to our system. Often our bodies, sensing that something is not right inside of us, search for ways to rebalance. This is an example of the ANS at work. To alleviate suffering and find that balance in the body, we must look at how all of these systems work together and find healing modalities that can address their specific needs.

OUR COMPLEX SET OF HORMONES

As women, our bodies produce four hormones that rise and fall throughout our monthly cycle—estrogen, testosterone, progesterone, and cortisol. Together they affect our mood, energy, memory, romantic life, habits, and cravings. Let's look at each of them separately.[11]

Estrogen

Estrogen is the primary female sex hormone, as well as our most powerful and most influential hormone when it comes to our behavior. Brizendine calls it the "Queen Hormone" because it can have a supreme reign over all our other hormones. It has a lot of influence over our other important mood-altering hormones and feel-good neurotransmitters such as serotonin and dopamine. As we age, our estrogen levels fluctuate and start to decline daily, weekly, and monthly, along with our moods. From adolescence to our postmenopause years, it heads our regulatory system. Estrogen can make us soft and alluring, but it can also have an aggressive component and has been shown to influence territorial behavior.

Progesterone

Progesterone is the hormone responsible for our menstrual cycles, but it also acts as a calming agent for the body. When working in tangent with allopregnanolone, progesterone can help calm us down. But this duo affects our energy in other ways. A drop in the levels of these two hormones, which happens right before our periods, can also give rise to the intense and frazzled feelings we call premenstrual syndrome or PMS.

Testosterone

Yes, women do have testosterone. And though we have considerably less than men, testosterone still gets the credit for those more typically male characteristics that make us feel powerful, assertive, aggressive, and, sometimes, lacking in compassion. It correlates to our ability to strengthen and maintain muscle mass. It is also associated with our sex drive, ability to orgasm, and overall sexual satisfaction. Studies show that as women age and testosterone decreases (it peaks in our early twenties and decreases about 10 percent every ten years after that), sexual complications can arise.[12] It can cause our libido to wane, and for some women the ability to create vaginal lubrication or achieve orgasm can be compromised. Testosterone is an important part of women's overall health as we age, especially when it comes to sexual satisfaction. We will go into this in more depth later in the book.

Cortisol

Finally we have cortisol, which provides our bodies with the energy to move if, suddenly, we need to. For example, if a bear is chasing you, cortisol will kick in and help you react quickly. Unfortunately, cortisol is also released when we are stressed or are experiencing emotional danger of some kind. And often, it does not turn off when it should, which means that if we find ourselves in an emotionally difficult situation for a long period of time, the extended release of cortisol can interfere with healthy endocrine function. This typically weakens our immune system which can lead to health problems, for example, backaches, headaches, insomnia, weight gain, and depression. Too much cortisol can overtax the brain and CNS, and reduce our ability to feel good or safe. Feeling safe plays a major role in our psychological health because it allows us to explore and enjoy our environment and other people without fear. As we will learn later, when we feel safe, we can truly be ourselves.

FEEL-GOOD NEUROTRANSMITTERS

Dr. Loretta Graziano Breuning, founder of the Inner Mammal Institute, calls these our "happy chemicals."[13] These neurotransmitters relay information to various cells located throughout the brain and body and are responsible for creating the different feelings and physical reactions that make us feel balanced and at peace. They also play a part in lesbian love addiction. Let's look at these neurotransmitters and the role they played in several lesbian love addicts.

Dopamine

A cluster of nerve cells lying underneath the cerebral cortex handles the release of dopamine, a powerful and complicated neurotransmitter and hormone that signals among many other things "reward" to the brain.[14] It is also well connected to the brain's pleasure center (yes, it's an actual place!), and it helps neurons communicate with one another. Dopamine is released when we experience romantic, sexual, and loving feelings, memories, and encounters.

Oxytocin

Another important hormone that guides us to connect, nurture, and make love is oxytocin. Oxytocin is released during kissing, touching, and sex. It is what turns on our feelings of intimacy and makes us want to cuddle. It is also the hormone that a mother's body produces when she breastfeeds her baby, which makes this important bonding experience pleasant for both mother and baby. Women produce a lot of this feel-good hormone, especially during romantic and sexual interactions. Now imagine two women together, both omitting this pleasurable chemical at the same time—it's an oxytocin fest! (If you wondered why lesbian sex can become so addicting for some women, here's your answer.)

On the night of Jane and Mary's first date, both of their brains omitted copious amounts of dopamine and oxytocin. Each woman felt high well before the date started, and just thinking of being together romantically released a cascade of this potent neurotransmitter. Each step of the way that night led them to higher levels of dopamine and oxytocin, and love addiction intoxication. After dinner, Jane and Mary drove around for hours unable to figure out what to do. Just being together in the car was so pleasurable that they didn't need anything more than to be next to each other. But large doses of dopamine and oxytocin also inhibit the prefrontal cortex, which might explain why they drove around aimlessly, and why neither woman could make a decision about what to do next. Ultimately, this led them back to Jane's couch.

Having sex that night released more dopamine and oxytocin. So did the countless texts that started the next day. Each time Jane received a text from Mary she got a mini hit of dopamine and oxytocin. Within days they were texting constantly and talking for hours every night.

Only five days after their first date, Mary sent Jane a text telling her that she had fallen in love with her. Of course, Jane was over the moon. When Jane had to go away for a weeklong business trip, both women feared they wouldn't survive being apart and counted the days until Jane got back. Before long they were sleeping at each other's place every night.

Serotonin

A major player in the neurotransmitter family, serotonin has a pivotal role in our mood and feelings of well-being. It coordinates the other hormones in our bodies and influences our appetite, sexual desire, sleep, memory, and learning ability. When we have enough serotonin, we feel good—balanced and happy. When the brain isn't producing enough, or our bodies are lacking the essential enzymes for adequate serotonin production, we may withdraw socially, or feel emotionally oversensitive and depressed. These feelings can also be brought on by the loss of a loved one. So, when women experience a painful loss, serotonin levels can drop dramatically, inducing feelings of depression, hopelessness, and fear. Many antidepressants are designed to augment serotonin levels and can be quite helpful in managing depression. Serotonin is also located in the gastrointestinal track, where it regulates intestinal movement, and throughout the CNS.

THE PLEASURE CENTER

Not surprisingly, our brain is hardwired to seek pleasure, both physical and psychological, which is why it prompts us to look for activities that we find enjoyable. The good news is, pleasurable activities are actually crucial to our survival; they help us live longer and encourage us to improve our circumstances.

Doing something we find pleasurable, such as connecting to other women, releases the all-powerful triad of serotonin, dopamine, and oxytocin throughout the brain's pleasure center. Cravings, pleasure, and fulfillment all come from the onslaught of these feel-good chemicals. The pleasure center also plays an important role in our understanding of lesbian love addiction because it is the place in the body where we create happiness, joy, contentment, fulfillment, and ecstasy.

When Matilda first met Sam she was immediately drawn to her. It was her eyes; she loved her eyes. Within days of meeting, the young women were texting constantly. They couldn't wait for their next chance to hang out. Within one month they were spending every night at each other's house, usually Matilda's. They felt so happy whenever they were together, and they both wanted more and more of each other. They fell into this blissful state for months.

When dopamine and oxytocin are released by our natural drive to connect, our pleasure center lights up, feelings of stress disappear, and our mood lightens. Life's struggles, painful memories, and self-esteem challenges seem to vanish.

Whenever Charley felt a spark with another woman she had just met her mood elevated just a little. She was not aware of this shift. All she understood was charming and seducing women was something she en-joyed—tremendously. Even when one did not call her back she had at least three more she was pursuing. This pattern of hitting on women kept her feel-good chemicals emitting pleasurable feelings, which kept Charley motivated.

Imagine two lesbians who are attracted to each other, getting physi-cal, and falling in love. Now picture an avalanche of dopamine and oxytocin being released in each of them, then passed back and forth and multiplying with each encounter. The high that each of these women get is a natural and healthy reaction—and what we all love about love! But for a love addict, this high is more like a heroin fix for a heroin addict. Over time the fix becomes more dangerous. Love addicts have a vulnerable pleasure system that can easily become overstimulated. And, as with any addiction over time, a tolerance builds and the craving for more grows insatiable. The brain goes through a series of changes that are set off by the anticipation of pleasure and finds its reward in com-pulsive or pleasure-seeking behavior. Once the addict is accustomed to this behavior, it can become impossible to stop.

Now we can see why Jane and Mary's and Matilda and Sam's honey-moon period was so pleasurable, so intense, and so intoxicating. The release of dopamine and oxytocin intensifies everything, creating a false sense of love, security, connection, and intimacy. In the following chap-ter we'll take a look at the different stages in a women's life cycle. We will also explore different attachment styles and how these components play a pivotal role in lesbian love addiction.

2

THE WAY WE CONNECT

[E]mpty without you.
— Eleanor Roosevelt to Lorena Hickok[1]

Now that we have looked at the basic components of the brain, this chapter will focus on how women connect. We'll achieve this by looking at the female life cycle and the various developmental stages, from infancy to womanhood. Then we'll explore the basic components of attachment theory that form in childhood and define the most common attachment types—secure, anxious, and avoidant—and how those affect our adult romantic relationships. Knowing about attachment styles can help you better understand your own romantic relationship patterns. We'll also look into how attachment influences lesbian love addiction.

THE FEMALE LIFE CYCLE

Returning back to Brizendine's work, let's take a quick look at a woman's life cycle in relation to our normal inclinations toward love, relationships, and heart connections. This is our nature—those beautiful parts we are born with that make us want to reach out to each other. We are born full of good intentions and understandable needs—unless something went wrong in utero and the wiring is damaged. When trauma occurs these natural inclinations can also be wounded. In this scenario, if a little girl (her nature) meets a difficult, shaming, boundary-less, and unwelcoming environment (her nurture), these fundamental ways of connecting are injured and love addiction can result.

In Utero

As the fetus develops, the area in the brain that houses our emotional center, where human relational behavior and the desire for connectedness resides, continues to grow. This area is also responsible for the verbal skills we need for processing our feelings and thoughts. For many women who are trying to heal, using these natural resources is crucial. Processing our experiences and feelings is a big part of healing. The drive to want to connect and communicate originates here.

Infancy

From the beginning, babies are compelled to study faces. This is how they first learn to make sense of the world visually. Baby girls are especially hardwired to participate in mutual gazing, looking directly at the adult face that is examining her own. Doing this helps the infant girl read and understand her primary caregiver, typically her mother. Please note, while the primary caregiver can come in various forms—biological mother, adoptive mother, grandmother, biological father, adoptive father, grandfather, foster parent—I will be using *mother* from this point forward, but this term is meant to be inclusive of all caretaking types. Think of it as who is doing the most "mothering."

During the first three months of life, an infant girl's ability to gaze into her mother's eyes and make contact increase by 400 percent! You can think of it as part of human evolution. Knowing her environment better and connecting with caretakers through mutual eye contact helps ensure her survival now and later.

For an infant, this is one of only a few ways to communicate with her caregiver, so she depends on the facial expressions and reactions of her mother to read what is going on around her. Studies have shown that infants have a difficult time with an unresponsive face, and that it often creates feelings of distress in the infant.

A well-known video demonstrates this perfectly: https://www.youtube.com/watch?v=apzXGEbZht0.[2] When you have a chance in the next day or so, take a moment to watch the video and pay attention to your feelings as you watch it. It might also be helpful to find a journal and write about your reactions after you finish watching the video.

In the staged experiment, a mother and her baby are interacting with one another. The mother makes cooing sounds, smiles, and holds the baby's hands, all the while maintaining eye contact with her daughter. As the mother talks to the baby, the baby responds by extending her arms and legs, making noises, and smiling. At times, she seems to be laughing, which makes the mother smile back at her. After a minute or so of this, everything changes, and the mother's face goes flat. Suddenly, the mother is expressionless. She stares at the baby, but makes no attempt to communicate verbally or to show any emotion or recognition of the baby's behavior. Soon the baby becomes distressed, and then starts to cry.

The video of the mother and infant demonstrates how an infant might interpret her mother's flat face negatively. Clearly, the mother has been asked by the researchers to change her expression dramatically, but the baby doesn't know this. She only knows that her mother has stopped interacting with her. Subsequently, the baby experiences the mother's silence and sudden flat face as complete abandonment. She starts to exhibit intense pain, as you'll see when you watch the video.

Because the baby also relates through vocal cues, the tone of a mother's voice plays an important role in an infant's feelings of safety and love. Evolutionarily speaking, listening to and interpreting her mother's vocal responses is another aspect of her survival. Thousands of years ago when humans were first forming, abandonment would mean certain death. So, if the infant's needs are not being met, the infant would learn how to tune into the mother's needs and figure out how to get them met by reading her moods. Despite our different world today, our brains are still wired to respond in this primal way. Our need for connection is the most natural thing in the world, and the joy we experience from that interaction is vital to our well-being.

EARLY ATTACHMENT

What happens during infancy plays a crucial role in our overall psychological makeup. If we examine infant behavior through the lens of attachment theory, we learn that psychological wounds can occur when the mother is not attuned to an infant's emotional needs. This can have a big impact even when basic needs are met—food, shelter, tempera-ture—but the emotional attunement is not there. That is because meet-ing basic needs is not enough. This is particularly evident when the mother does not know how to respond to her baby's emotional needs in a way that fits that girl's individual temperament. Eye gazing and facial recognition is vital to the infant girl's development, and by meeting this biological need with warm, physical, and verbal responses, the mother contributes to an emotional well-being that can set the stage for life. When the mother and other close family members attune to the verbal and nonverbal responses she uses to communicate her emotional needs, the infant girl will begin to develop a healthy sense of herself. This is because she experiences others *enjoying* her, *loving* her, and *connecting* to her for who she is. In fulfilling her biological need for connection, we give her the message that she is worthy of the positive attention she is receiving. Later we will look at what happens when the child does not receive consistent, warm, or loving attention.

The next two years are also pivotal for the infant's development into toddlerhood. At this stage, a child will continue to attune to her sur-rounding environment in more sophisticated ways while her nervous system will absorb her mother's energy in a greater degree. This may seem obvious in our more psychologically educated society, but it wasn't that long ago that researchers did not have the data to illustrate how a mother's internal state affects her daughter's internal state. A girl raised by an even-tempered and emotionally available mother in a stable environment is more likely to become a similarly calm, stable person as she grows.

Mary

Mary's mother, while she loved her daughter, was challenged by Mary's early, more temperamental years. She had an idealized view of mother-hood and expected raising young children to be an easier experience. She was ambivalent about Mary's typical bids for attention and autono-my and her temper tantrums. She began to think of Jane as "difficult"— a label that still exists in her family to this day. Her mother also suffered from anxiety, but she was not diagnosed and treated until much later in her life. Mary didn't realize how much living with her mother's anxiety affected her until she started lesbian-affirmative therapy and received treatment for her love addiction.

Many of us are aware of how stress influences our health, but it's important to recognize the negative effect that a stressful environment can have on children. A mother who lives with a lot of stress in her life and is often worried and anxious can have a much harder time nurturing her daughter. When our ACC is extremely active, it can take over, making it harder for a mother to be her own authentic self and create a calm environment for her daughter.

Nancy Chodorow wrote extensively on the ambivalence most mothers have toward their daughters. Her 1978 book, *The Reproduction of Mothering*,[3] looked at the mother-daughter relationship and changed the landscape of psychology by opening up the way therapists' viewed female development. Chodorow discovered that the dynamic between mother and daughter was more complex than first imagined by psychology's forefathers such as Freud. She examined a mother's natural conflict around her daughter's need for both autonomy and connection due to her own unresolved issues. Being the same sex, the mother's chances for projecting her own needs onto the daughter are greater than toward a son—who is naturally experienced as different. This ambivalence sends mixed messages to the daughter who becomes confused when to take care of herself and when to take care of her mother. This can also have a negative effect on a little girl's budding sense of self.

BEYOND OUR YOUNG CHILDHOOD: THE NEXT DEVELOPMENT YEARS

Young Girls

The young girl will continue to learn how others relate to her and to understand herself by interpreting people's facial expressions, touch, and emotional reactions. It is in this context that the girl begins to see herself through the eyes of others, especially her mother and other close family members. It is common for girls to enjoy attuning to others because they find the way people express themselves fascinating. Social and emotional interactions and behaviors are naturally interesting to us. You could say that it is our brain doing its job.

Young girls are also very dependent on their mothers. The relationship that lesbians have with their mother as children is paramount. Because we are naturally drawn to members of our own sex, our early interactions with the important women in our lives imprint themselves on our psyches. How we relate to our mother as a child has a lasting effect on our self-esteem and sense of self. We'll discuss the influence that mothers have on their lesbian daughters in more depth in chapter 3.

During the late childhood stage, gender expression may become more obvious. Girls may develop tomboyish qualities or show an interest in and aptitude for sports. Others invest their energy into school and getting good grades and prefer books to competitive sports. Keep in mind, lesbians exhibit a wide range of interests and gender expressions, from typically feminine to androgynous, to tomboyish or more masculine traits. I say this to avoid adding to lesbian stereotypes, which are dangerous for obvious reasons.

Those who fall outside of culturally accepted norms of gender expression and behavior may find this to be a rough time. Many parents can be hypercritical of their daughters, especially those who find themselves worried about their daughter's difference, or are threatened by her willingness to stand apart from gender conventions. Feminine lesbians can easily fall under the radar at this age, and continue to be fed stereotypical heterocentric ideals and fairytale narratives about meeting their Prince Charming and living happily ever after. These gendered narratives can cause sexual orientation confusion later when girls' budding romantic interests and sexual identities are emerging.

This particular issue is beginning to change with the help of social movements that have drawn more awareness to the harm of gender stereotypes and have insisted on providing girls with new role models in the media. Organizations that target the media's portrayal of girls in children's stories and comics, such as the nonprofit organization Geena Davis Institute on Gender in Media (http://seejane.org/), are moving things forward. More recently, there has been a surge in less stereotypical fairytale stories such as Disney's *Frozen* and Angelina Jolie's *Maleficent*. Each of these movies feature strong female heroines with strong bonds and relationships between women. As these narratives continue to evolve, younger generations will benefit from the awareness, and those who grew up in a less evolved world benefit from this paradigm shift. I recommend using all the information you are gathering now to rewrite your own story, in your own words. Doing this is a powerful remedy for the trauma inflicted by narrow gender stereotypes.

Lesbians who grew up prior to the influence the feminist and gay liberation movements have on the media today will recall a more sexist and heterocentric era when the reality of women loving women was invisible in pop culture and history courses. Before the postfeminist period, it wasn't as common for girls to be formally taught the extent to which women contributed to history and civilization. Women's roles were largely defined by being wives and mothers. The millennials, who are growing up in a culture influenced by feminism and the LGBTQ liberation movement, may not realize that women weren't always as prominent as they seem to be now. Women did not hold many positions of power, and typical history classes almost never taught about women who influenced the world. The positive impact on cultural values that these advances have on the media, on education, and our daily lives and relationships should not be underestimated.

It is not as if girls don't continue to face sexism and pressure to conform to gender stereotypes today. Women are still measured according to how white, slim, beautiful, and attractive to men they are. Period. *An adolescent girl who doesn't adhere to gender norms can find this a very exciting time and/or a very terrifying experience.* Self-esteem continues to be a great challenge for girls, especially in the initial stages of puberty, and gender-identity struggles can make this life transition even more so. Let's look at one example of how these early experiences can affect us as adults.

Charley

By age eleven, Charley already knew she was attracted to girls. Charley, a 55-year-old bitch lesbian, grew up in a liberal, open-minded Jewish household, and because her parents were very progressive, she expected them to respond with understanding when she came out. She was not at all prepared for her mother's extremely negative reaction. Like many parents, Charley's were fine with the idea of people being LGBT—as long as their daughter was not one of them. Her mother's rejection was devastating. Since she had spent most of her childhood seeking her mother's love and approval, this marked a final abandonment. This experience at eleven years of age not only made for an awkward entryway into Charley's adolescence, it created a deep wound that led to other more difficult challenges later in life. Among them, being vulnerable to the modus operandi of a sexual predator, as well as a forty-year battle with sex and love addiction.

Adolescent

As Charley's story demonstrates, adolescence can be one of the most difficult times in a young woman's life, in particular how it influences identity. Many lesbians feel extremely vulnerable during this time in their development, and the insecurity that arises can cause a great deal of internal stress. As puberty sets in, this feeling of insecurity seems to be the norm as the body is undergoing many important changes.

The first of these is the flood of sex hormones into the system, which can lead to psychological confusion and the development of a critical inner voice that begins to dominate thoughts. These hormones are also responsible for the development of secondary sex characteristics such as breasts, hips, thighs, and pubic hair. Overall, this is a time of great transformation. Menstruation starts. Sexual and romantic desires develop. While their bodies are preparing biologically to bear children, psychologically girls are not at all ready for the complexities of romantic relationships, let alone the responsibility of having children.

For many girls, this period is dominated by concerns about their looks, how well they interact with others, and peer positioning—knowing who is liked or disliked by whom. This time is often overwhelming because the prefrontal cortex, which helps us understand and regulate our emotional selves, is not yet developed. This means that the limbic system often takes control. Feeling anxious, angry, and entitled are not uncommon. It is understandably a hard time in a girl's life. It can also be difficult on the entire family as the parents try to figure out how to handle a young woman who is plagued by raging hormones and emotions, yet with little foresight.

COMING OUT

This is about the time some lesbians start to realize that they are attracted to members of the same sex, or develop a faint understanding that they are not interested in boys in the same way many of their friends are. They may find themselves captivated by a female friend, but they don't yet recognize those feelings as romantic.

There are also lesbians who first become aware of their same-sex attraction in their early twenties or thirties. Many lesbians struggle with the coming out process. Some do not. Some don't feel comfortable labeling their sexual identity for years. Some do initially come out as bisexual to later realize they are interested only in other women. Some, of course, are bisexual their entire lives. Whatever the situation, it is a process. Coming out is a complex, personal experience, which is different for everyone. There is no right or wrong way. For the lesbian who is vulnerable to love addiction, characteristics start to form just as their interest in romance and sex arises. For others, the coming out experience is so liberating, a high all of its own, that love addiction traits (that might turn into a full-blown love addiction) erupt just as one's true self is finally known.

SEXUAL ASSAULT

One in four women will be sexually assaulted in her lifetime.[4] One in four. That means that for every four girls or women in the United States, one of them either is or will be a victim of sexual assault, perpetrated by a parent, family member, sibling, teacher, mentor, friend, date, or stranger. The unfortunate reality is that we are vulnerable to predators, pedophiles, or rapists at any time—during childhood or adolescence, or as teens or adults. It can happen to a very young girl or during the high school and college years, where drinking and date rape often coexist. Whether she is heterosexual, bisexual, fluid, or lesbian doesn't matter to the predator. Many girls are targeted when they are young and barely aware of their sexuality.

LESBIANS AND SEXUAL ASSAULT

Studies show that 21 percent of lesbians have been sexually abused as children and 15 percent were sexually assaulted as adults[5] (which falls into the statistic of one in four). Most importantly, there is no causal relationship between childhood sexual abuse or assault and being a lesbian. Unfortunately, too many people believe that sexual assault turns a girl into a lesbian, despite no evidence supporting this. Ignorance and homophobic attitudes are usually the source of this misinformation. However, the trauma of sexual assault can cause addictive and destructive behaviors.

More often than not, girls who have been sexually abused or assaulted do not get the help and support they need during or after the assault. In fact, many women and girls don't even report rape or sexual abuse because of shame, self-blame, and fear of retaliation from the perpetrator. They blame themselves for the incident, and without a safe person or place to disclose this information, the trauma goes untreated, sometimes for decades. Unfortunately, Charley was one of those girls who became a victim of sexual assault at a young age, and the trauma she experienced left her vulnerable to sex and love addiction later in her life. It is also one of the more common reasons for young women to turn, unconsciously, to substance abuse to push away the pain. This is another part of Charley's story.

Charley, a 55-year-old bitch lesbian, grew up poor. Her family moved around a lot and had few resources. As a child, Charley was never offered a good explanation for why the family had to move so often, but she was aware that they had lost several of their houses and that her father's gambling and the stress this put on the family played a part. Having been abandoned emotionally by her mother when she came out to her at age eleven, Charley was an emotionally neglected tomboy who felt very different from most of her peers. When she was fifteen years old, she developed a friendship with an adult male in her family. She was vulnerable, and the distant relationship with her parents meant she had little oversight or guidance. She knew nothing about predators. Even though she knew she was a lesbian, the attention this man gave her felt good, and it filled a deep need in her to connect with someone.

THE PLEASURE IN CONNECTION

During adolescence, the brain's pleasure center is developing and is increasingly activated by interpersonal communication and connection. Talking makes us feel good, and at this developmental stage, talking about sex and romantic experiences like love stimulates oxytocin and dopamine production in a new and dazzling way. Brizendine describes it best:

> We are not talking about a small amount of pleasure. This is huge. It's a major dopamine and oxytocin rush, which is the biggest, fattest neurological reward you can get outside of an orgasm.[6]

It's no wonder we need to connect and exchange ideas. Talking and being part of a conversation feeds our brains as much as it feeds our imagination.

It is no wonder Charley ended up in a dangerous relationship. Living with parents who essentially shunned her, and being ignored and treated as an outsider among her peers, Charley needed someone to talk to, someone who might understand her. She found that someone in a male figure who established an inappropriate relationship with her. This man was one of the only people in Charley's life who gave her attention. She was intrigued by him, and the way that he engaged her in conversation about beautiful women, a subject that was off limits with other people Charley loved. She felt better after spending time with him. Once he introduced her to the subject of sex, all bets were off. Wham—her pleasure centers were hooked.

As stated earlier, the prefrontal cortex is the last part of the brain to develop and is the part of the brain that assesses a situation and makes decisions based on safety and logic. It ideally protects us from harm, helps us pause our desires and impulses, and guides us with wisdom. This means that fifteen-year-old Charley was being seduced by a man she trusted, in part because she was not yet old enough to understand the gravity of the situation. It would take many years, sobriety from alcoholism, and a twelve-step program for sex and love addiction before she could stand back and assess the situation accurately.

The man Charley befriended spent a long time grooming her, gradually building her trust, then he introduced her to sex, using her attraction to other girls as bait. To bond with her, he made checking out beautiful women together a ritual. Eventually he introduced her to heterosexual porn. Looking at porn aroused Charley, and she began to enjoy seeing women used for sex. The image of women as sex objects became embedded in the pleasure centers of her brain. Eventually, he raped her. This continued for years.

No one in Charley's family seemed bothered that she was too young to be hanging out with a man his age. This is not uncommon in families that are emotionally neglectful. Even though she wanted to be sexual with women, his attention proved irresistible since she was starved for love. Charley was psychologically seduced and bonded with her perpetrator in a way similar to Stockholm syndrome (the victim begins to identify with the assailant and develops positive, even idealized, feelings toward them). She began to trust him, despite the psychological and emotional damage he was causing her. He exploited her attraction to women by using them to get and keep her interest. As Charley's awareness of the inappropriate and unhealthy nature of this relationship grew, she became paralyzed by fear and confusion about how to stop it. She not only feared rejection, she worried that if she told her family, they would blame her.

Like many women in abusive situations, Charley kept it a secret, which compounded the shame she felt. She blamed herself for having sex with him, and blamed herself for enjoying aspects of it. Charley was unable to see how he had manipulated her and her innocence. Charley finally removed him from her life when she moved to a different city in her twenties. By then, however, the damage was done, and the experience was imprinted in her brain. It left her unable to be turned on by anything other than women as sex objects. She was addicted to porn, and thought watching it on a daily basis was normal. She had no idea how to be in a healthy relationship, and her sex and love addiction was all-consuming.

ATTACHMENT THEORY

If we look at Charley's experiences from the perspective of attachment theory, we can understand them from a different angle. As we learned in the introduction, attachment theory looks at the way infants behave and bond with their mothers. Researchers have developed a number of attachment styles, which are based on the relational patterns that infants exhibit in their mother's presence, compared with their behavior in the presence of a stranger.

The Strange Situation Experiment

In an experimental procedure created by developmental psychologist Mary Ainsworth, researchers interviewed mothers when they were pregnant, and later on when their babies were between six to eighteen months old. The study, called *The Strange Situation*, was a close and detailed observation of how these infants behaved in a number of situations: alone, with the mother, and with an unfamiliar person. What the researchers found was groundbreaking, and much of today's parenting theories and styles have been influenced by these findings.

The researchers developed several categories based on the infant's reactions to the mother's absence, and used them to organize and explain their findings. The infant responses were measured and categorized by a range of behaviors and ways of relating, from secure to insecure, that served as indicators of the proposed attachment styles they were developing. Interestingly, the data shows that these attachment styles are similar across cultures. Since these experiments were first conducted in the 1970s, psychologists have come to understand that these styles are not as fixed as Ainsworth had first imagined. More recent findings show us that the child's relationship with the mother is not the only one that matters. It turns out that there are several other important human connections that influence a child's attachment style over time. However, the initial relationship with the mother has a deep and lasting impact on our way of relating to other human beings throughout our lives.

The Four Attachment Styles

Secure

This is considered the optimal state and indicates that a child is securely attached to the mother and, consequently, experiences that feeling of security internally. This infant may be upset when the mother initially leaves, but the upset is naturally resolved when the infant begins to interact with the environment or a known family member, babysitter, or caregiver at a daycare center or preschool. Securely attached babies are happy to see their mothers when they return and immediately interact with them. Once again in the mother's arms, the infant becomes content and able to focus on the surrounding environment. A secure attachment to the mother allows the child to feel safe and, therefore, to focus on her external environment where she learns and grows. This is the ideal situation that can set the stage for secure and happy relationships as adults. Insecure attachment styles fall into three categories.

Anxious-Resistant

Infants with anxious-resistant, or ambivalent, behavior are leery of strangers even in the presence of their mother and often display ambivalence toward the mother when she returns. The studies indicate that these infants are usually subject to unpredictable parenting—the mother responds in a warm and sensitive manner some of the time, and at other times she does not. This unpredictability pushes the infant to behave in ways that offer them control, such as resisting the mother's bid for closeness when she returns to the room.

Anxious-Avoidant

This infant shows little signs of distress when the mom leaves or returns. Sometimes the infant will act indifferent or angry, but they are very protective of themselves and show avoidance of the stranger when left with that person. Studies indicate that the anxious-avoidant child's emotional needs may not have been adequately met. Consequently, a type of hopelessness sets in. They are indifferent to the mother when she returns. Though it may seem as if this child is not bothered by the difference, data suggests that they are internally distressed.

See the index for links to videos to see these studies in action.[7]

Disorganized

This is the most distressed of all styles. A disorganized infant shows unusual or disoriented behavior in the stranger situation. Head-cocking, jerking movements, extreme forms of fear, distracted, and detached behaviors are not uncommon. Infants who display this behavior often came from violent or abusive households. They may have tragically encountered sexual trauma in infancy.

We will look at examples of the ways in which these styles manifest in adulthood, particularly in romantic relationships. As you can imagine, a range of insecure attachment styles can be present for lesbians suffering from love addiction.

ADULTHOOD—FINDING A MATE

Adulthood, for many lesbians, is defined by our interest and desire in finding a mate. The challenging years of the early adolescence are over, and our prefrontal cortex matures by the age of twenty-five.[8] College, careers, and, possibly creating a family become important. This time is when dating and falling in love usually take priority. While some young lesbians move into adulthood with foresight and grace, those suffering from any kind of addiction can find themselves emotionally delayed. This is especially true about relationship choices and behaviors when love addiction occurs. Some lesbians have co-occurring addictions such as alcoholism and love addition. This can make it harder to diagnose love addiction because heavy drinking impairs decision making, which influences relationship choices. Addictions hold a lesbian back from creating a more stable and productive life. For a love addict, this is most pronounced in her love life. Charley's story is a good illustration of that.

Charley eventually met her future wife. They fell in love and quickly moved in together. As is often the case in love addiction, the honeymoon period ended too quickly, and they fell into a boring and disconnecting ritual of coupledom. Around this time, Charley's alcoholism became uncontrollable, and she found herself in rehab. Thankfully, she took to sobriety immediately, and when she returned home she became active in Alcoholics Anonymous and life got better for a while. But their sex life was sporadic at best. Charley, an anxious type, began protesting about the lack of sex and communication, and because of her trauma she came across as needy and insatiable. Charley remained in this unsatisfying relationship for fifteen years because she reunited with her old friends—porn and flirting.

ADULT ATTACHMENT STYLES

Our attachment styles play a huge role in our lives. Now you can understand how our attachment styles are deeply influenced by our mother's style of relating and parenting. Even as adults, the relationships we developed with our mother, father, caregivers, siblings, other family members, and friends impacts us, despite the relationship starting decades ago. Research shows those early years are of paramount importance to how we relate as adults despite our resilience and ability to change.

In psychotherapy, we can use family-of-origin work or psychodynamic work to revisit our childhood and find the origins of our trauma. The idea is not to stay stuck in blaming your parents. Chances are they were doing the best they could with the tools, or lack thereof, they had at the time. The intention of the work is to realize the point of dislocation or loss and the wound it may have created. Our early developmental challenges are pivotal to our budding sense of self, our feelings of security and well-being, and our self-regard. Visiting our roots can provide a reason for our suffering, and show us what may have influenced our decisions in love and in life. It can help us understand the inner critic deep inside our minds and show us how it got there. Eventually, when the trauma is healed, we forgive our parents and move on, taking responsibility for our own lives. However, the healing must take place before that can happen, and understanding the origin of the challenging or confusing aspects of yourself is a productive place to start.

In 2010 Dr. Amir Levine and Rachel S. F. Heller brought many of the complex attachment studies and applied them to adult relationships in *Attached: The New Science of Adult Attachment and How It Can Help You Find—and Keep—Love.*[9] The book synthesizes Bowlby and Ainsworth's theories, focusing on secure, anxious, and avoidant attachment styles and exploring how these styles shape the ability to love and be loved. As usual, the narrative is heterocentric and only uses heterosexual relationships to illustrate attachment concepts but is still helpful to examine here. That is why I am excited to incorporate their work into this book so that we, as lesbians, can use this important information while at the same time see our lesbianism mirrored in ways that are helpful.

For these purposes, I will use their research to help me summarize how these three secure, anxious, and avoidant styles manifest in adults. Another term developed by Levine and Heller, the *super-sensitive attachment system*,[10] is a helpful descriptor of how someone with an insecure attachment—in our case a lesbian love addict—becomes activated, displaying anxious or avoidant behaviors.

The following information should help you identify how your attachment style influences your relationship patterns. For the link to a validated online test created by Dr. Chris Farley that helps you determine your style, go to http://www.web-research-design.net/cgi-bin/crq/crq.pl.[11] There are also a number of attachment tests in *Attached*, which I also recommend. Either before or after the test, you'll find these explanations helpful.

Later, in chapter 5, we'll take a more detailed look at how these various styles show up in lesbian love addiction.

Secure

A securely attached lesbian feels naturally happy when in a relationship. Faithful, reliable, accountable, reasonable, and loving, she is available and enjoys both emotional and sexual intimacy with her partner. Because of her secure attachment she does not become preoccupied or feel the need to flee from her partner. She believes her partner when she says she loves her and trusts her to be faithful. She spends her day focusing on what she needs to focus on, whether it's work, family, or recreation. Research shows that securely attached individuals report higher levels of contentment in their relationships than their insecure counterparts. They also report being happier and more fulfilled in their lives in general.

Tanya

Tanya, a forty-year-old African American soft butch lesbian, who had a kind and generous spirit, was securely attached. She was reliable and consistent, supportive, loving, and affectionate and had a healthy sex drive. She and her partner, also African American, had been together for five years and were still in love. She did not question her partner's love for her and was actively engaged in the life they had created together. Though each was securely attached, they still had their own trauma (including institutionalized racism and lesbianphobia) they brought to the relationship, which did cause a fight or disagreement from time to time. On a couple of those occasions they had to take a few days break—a "time out," so to speak—before they could talk and work out their differences. Those breaks gave each of them time to calm down, go to their therapist, twelve-step program, pastor, or friend for clarity. Once they were calm and had processed their triggers, they would reconnect and talk it through. They didn't always find the ideal resolution or compromise, but the repair process usually brought them closer.

Anxious

As the name implies, this lesbian worries—a lot. She is consistently fearful and preoccupied with her partner's level of interest because she looks for signs of disinterest or a decline in the connection. She is basically on high alert, interpreting the slightest lack of response as a sign of problems. She may also need a lot of reassurance from her partner that everything is okay and she is still loved. An anxious type will interpret her partner's inability to text or call her right back as a sign of impending doom. If she sends a text and does not receive a response immediately, the rest of her day can be spent catastrophizing the relationship or demonizing her partner. She is often acting from anger and believes that her anxiety is the fault of her partner, who she thinks should always provide a swift response and reassurance.

Julie

Julie suffered from anxiety. She did not like to be alone and was unhappy whenever she was single. In her latest relationship, still in its first year, she found herself thinking of her girlfriend nonstop. She wanted to be with her all the time. Since her girlfriend was busy with a career and life she had developed long before they met, Julie felt anxious often. Intellectually she understood her girlfriend was busy and was not going to drop everything to be with her, but over time she found herself catastrophizing her girlfriend's healthy need for autonomy. If she didn't hear back from her within an hour of reaching out, thoughts of being abandoned by her would take over her rational mind. This would escalate Julie to confront Sandra, asking her where she was and why she wasn't texting her back. These anxious episodes were the result of Julie's super-sensitive attachment system. Once activated, Julie was unable to calm herself down until her girlfriend had reassured her they were fine. She started to realize that if she didn't get some help she would ruin this relationship, just as she had many others.

Avoidant

This lesbian usually values self-sufficiency above all else. Afraid of being suffocated or smothered or losing her independence in a relationship, she is never truly available to her partner. The intensity of the early romantic phase gives a false sense of intimacy to both women, but once the honeymoon phase is over, the avoidant's need for independence overrides their initial closeness. Affection and sex diminish. She rationalizes these changes as an important part of her "independent spirit." Even if she decides to stay in the relationship, she may use criticism to further distance herself. This can go on for years. She will feel alone even when in a relationship and often long to be out of it, forgetting how lonely she was when she was single. She romanticizes past romances (even those that were awful) and often intrigue with others while in a relationship. Avoidants are chronically dissatisfied with their romantic life. Ambivalence is their closest friend. Their behavior can be extremely challenging to their partners (especially if they are an anxious type), and loneliness often becomes the hallmark for both involved.

Sophie

Sophie was charming and smart. She was popular and had no problem meeting women. Even though she was in a committed relationship, she had recently found herself flirting with a new girl at work. She knew it was wrong, but her girlfriend, Monica, had been getting on her nerves lately and she enjoyed the idea that there were other potential women out there in case this relationship did not work out. Fiercely independent, she was afraid to take the next step and move in, although Monica had been pushing her to do it for a while now. Monica was tired of living in two places. She wanted the relationship to go to the next level and had even started hinting at marriage, especially since it had just become legal in their state. Sophie started to feel smothered and didn't have any idea how she was going to move in with Monica, let alone marry her. Historically, when in this position, Sophie found herself flirting with other women while simultaneously pulling away. She just wasn't that turned on by Monica anymore. She couldn't understand why this kept happening to her. Another coworker, knowing Sophie's past, suggested she go to therapy. Sophie was thinking about calling the number her friend had just given her. She was recognizing a pattern she wasn't too thrilled about.

WHAT'S NEXT?

Brizendine's work raises awareness about the ways in which women are biologically wired to connect. Attachment theory illustrates how a mother's psychological well-being and ability to meet her infant daughter's emotional temperament and needs affect the girl's future romantic relationships. When we apply these concepts to the unique characteristics of lesbian relationships, we can look more closely at the potential for positive and negative consequences. We will integrate each of these pieces of lesbian love addiction and fully explore its impact as we move through the book. Our next chapter will take a closer look at how growing up in a heterocentric and homophobic society contributes to lesbian love addiction.

3

WHAT IS UNIQUE ABOUT LESBIAN LOVE ADDICTION?

> She didn't get mad
> She didn't even cry
> She lit a cigarette
> Then she said goodbye
> I must have missed a sign
> I missed a turn somewhere
> When I looked in her eyes
> There was a stranger there.

—"When a Woman Goes Cold," —Mary Gauthier[1]

You might be wondering why lesbian love addiction is different from the love addiction straight, gay men, bisexual, or any other set of people face. The short answer to that very important question is that the lesbian psyche, which has its own unique characteristics. Our sexuality—and who we love—informs so much of who we are from childhood on into adulthood. It profoundly shapes our identities, our life experiences, the relationships we have with our main attachment figures, and ultimately, our sense of self. By looking at the lesbian psyche from a lesbian-affirmative perspective, we begin to understand some of the unique issues facing women who love women—and how this affects the way we love ourselves.

Of course, there are many traits that we all share as addicts, many of which we will continue to learn from, but this chapter is going to focus on love addiction as it relates to the key components of the lesbian psyche. Lesbians are impacted by the heterocentric world in a way that is different from what nonlesbian women and all men experience. Understanding why these distinctions matter is part of the healing process for lesbians who battle love addiction.

WHY WE ARE UNIQUE

I certainly know what it is like to grow up lesbian, from my own experience and from the stories I hear every day from my patients and students. Throughout my career, one important point has become increasingly clear to me that I believe is fundamental to our understanding of the lesbian experience. Regardless of your experience coming out, whether you were aware of being a lesbian or bisexual when you were very young (some of us knew, some of us didn't) or whether you came out in high school or in your thirties, whether you experimented with men or were once married to a man and had children with him, all lesbians have a common denominator. We all grew up in a world that repeatedly erased our history and our legacies and forced us to fight for fundamental human rights such as marriage equality, and we all share the historical and cultural experience of invisibility, of living with shame, and being treated with bias and contempt.

Let me clarify something important here. While I am offering a particularly critical view of our current environment, I don't mean to paint an entirely bleak portrait. In many ways, cultural attitudes toward same-sex love have improved dramatically, and it is comforting to know that the LGBTQ equality movement is one of the fastest growing social justice movements in history.[2] In June 26, 2015, when the Supreme Court's 5-4 ruling gave same-sex couples the right to marry in all fifty states, it will be remembered as one of the most important days in the LGBTQ equality movement. I am grateful for this progress. Still, acknowledging that we even had to fight for the right to marry, and ultimately to have parity with heterosexuals is an undeniable problem. With every backlash, such as the 2015 Indiana law, the Religious Freedom Restoration Act, which first allowed businesses to discriminate against LGBTQ folks, it is heartening to see people responding with a nationwide protest,[3] but continuing to engage in these troubling debates about our rights as citizens is tiring and wrong. Being denied the basic human right to live our lives loving the people we choose is unacceptable at this point in our evolution. The prejudice we continue to face is traumatizing for all of us. Even when the victories feel amazing, we know that the work is far from done. Despite these exciting and life-altering societal shifts, thousands of years of oppression and discrimination has deeply affected how we feel about ourselves on the inside.

This is an essential truth that I want to pass on. It is easy to believe that our psychological stories began with our coming out, when in reality they began long before that. Our lesbian stories really begin when we were very young children living with our families and taking in cultural messages from them and the world around us. All of these messages we received were seen and experienced from a child's perspective. In the same way that we explored the female brain and attachment theories in previous chapters, we will now look at how a hetero-centric society, one that reveres the white, heterosexual male, that sees and teaches everything from a heterosexual perspective, and sanctifies heterosexual privilege, profoundly affects the lesbian psyche as it is developing.

By now you know that our attachment to our mothers and our relationship with our families shape who we become and have a powerful effect on the relationship we have with ourselves. These primary relationships can often be the first place where we engage with phobic or negative messages about who we are. While many of us are unaware of their existence growing up, we still respond to and internalize these messages without being aware of the harm they are causing.

Negative internalized messages can be very potent and destructive to our sense of self, particularly when they take the form of self-hatred and harsh self-criticism. They live inside of us and show up in our negative self-talk and are our inner critic. Those conversations we have with ourselves that no one else can hear. Low self-esteem and an unforgiving internal voice are especially insidious and damaging because they are often so deeply buried that we don't even recognize them. This is similar to the inner critic that appears in adolescence, which I touched on in chapter 2. As young women develop a stronger understanding of the world around them, they are also vulnerable to the negative self-talk that increases during this stage of life.

Matilda was a young, white, upper-middle-class lesbian. She had grown up in a large family with five siblings. Her father was a successful workaholic who was emotionally distant and critical of his children. When he walked into a room, everyone tensed up. The family was afraid of him. Matilda's mother had been an alcoholic for many years, and this created family problems that were never addressed. The addiction made her very unpredictable, giving Matilda love and attention one moment, then ignoring her the next. She shared her personal problems with Matilda in inappropriate ways, treating her like a friend rather than a daughter. Because her mother was often drunk, Matilda was left to care for her younger brothers and sisters and was overburdened by adult responsibilities too early in her life. In psychological jargon we call this being *parentified*.

Even before Matilda was aware of her sexuality, she knew that she was different from the other members of her family. Her parents were conservative, and her father had made it clear that he was not okay with same-sex relationships. Matilda could not figure out why she felt different from others. She only knew that both of her parents were critical of her. By the time she became a teenager, an unflinching inner critic had taken residence inside of her. Years later in therapy, she gave the inner critic a name—the bully.

As a psychologist, I am aware of the impact that being different can have on a person's sense of belonging. Living outside of societal norms carries with it extra sadness and stress, which can make our relationships more complicated. Navigating our differences can be a huge challenge on its own, but adding love addiction to the mix makes it even tougher. Even when we are an out and proud lesbian, the pain and stress that is part of our inner psychic experience can make it that much harder to function or thrive in our work, our relationships, and our daily lives. Unfortunately, the reality is that we live in a homophobic world, and we take in that phobia whether or not we are aware of it. This extra load can weigh heavily on us, and compromise our overall happiness.

Those of us who live in bigger, more progressive cities and areas of the United States are not exempt from these negative messages. We may think that we're safe because we live in San Francisco, Los Angeles, or New York, but the homophobic messages we absorbed when we were young and growing up are still present within us. Lesbians who live in those areas where homophobia is more pronounced, who are closeted to their families or employers or town members, need to hear this too. Growing up in a world that is unaccepting or dismissive of who we are as human beings is traumatizing. Period.

THE QUASHED LESBIAN SENSE OF SELF

Lesbians can be some of the most traumatized people in the world. I do not say this lightly, nor is it my intention to bring shame to lesbians. The trauma is not our fault. It is a by-product of living in an intolerant and judgmental world, and of growing up in a misogynistic, sexist, and homophobic culture. It bears restating that in addition to being sexual minorities, we are women, and this means that we have been shaped by a world that not only devalues and oppresses women, but one that is blatantly homophobic. Affirmative therapists call this phenomenon *double trauma*[4] because we are women and lesbians both, and it is impossible to squeak through life without being affected by messages that demean us. As young women and girls, our psyches take everything in, and none of us are impervious to the messages we absorb from a heterocentric, heterosexist, and racist culture. Even if we didn't experience misogyny or homophobia directly, they existed in the phrases we heard on the playground at school, in the off-color comments of our relatives and peers, and the subtle statements made in the media, movies, and television shows. They have always been there, bearing down even on the strongest of us, injuring our vulnerable, developing sense of self.

Most of us can recall a moment or two from our childhood when we first realized that people around us considered girls less valuable. It may have been communicated in your family, when the new baby arrived and you remember how excited people seemed that it was a boy. It may have been the silly but hurtful things they said to you about being a girl, or how your family members paid more attention to the boys, or treated them with more seriousness and respect even in the most subtle of ways. It may have been in a social situation, or at school when a bully said something derogatory about your girl parts or breasts. We store these experiences, and over time they chip away at us.

LESBIANS OF COLOR

Similar to the concept of double trauma, the threat that lesbians of color face originates from several oppressive systems. The most obvious of these is racism. Because the color of one's skin is typically what people notice first, gender and gender expression are second and third in line. Put simply, the triple threat to white male privilege would be an African American, Asian, or Latina lesbian who identifies as butch. Whether or not their sexuality and gender expressions are obvious, lesbians of color face a racist and homophobic society. From the affirmative perspective this type of trauma is called *multiple oppression*.[5] This, in addition to living within a community or belonging to a faith that is LGBTQ-phobic, can erode a woman of color's sense of self over time. Being part of a social or religious community that promotes homophobia is not only harmful, it puts a lot of pressure on lesbians who feel forced to choose between the family of origin and family of choice because the two worlds are unable to come together.[6] This can be very stressful and difficult to negotiate. The lack of awareness about these issues is often the source of division among the LGBTQ community, many of whom argue that race and gender are the great separators. But again, it also creates great resilience.

As we learned in chapter 1 on development, our brains are wired to attune socially, and we learn to understand ourselves in part by reading and interpreting the way other people experience us. So when we receive hurtful and hateful messages, whether they are covert or overt, it is nearly impossible for our young minds to reject them, or see them as false. Developmentally, children don't have the cognitive ability to discern in that way. Their minds are like sponges. They don't know how to question the ideas that the adult world presents to them or how to shield themselves from the negative messages that threaten their self-esteem. Instead, children hear or experience something unpleasant and internalize it and often perceive it as a truth. A young girl notices the way people who are different are treated, and she may end up doing everything she can to be like everyone else to avoid standing out from the crowd.

A young mind may begin to believe that these horrible missives about "homosexuals" are true even if we don't know we are lesbians yet. We see that lesbians are not okay, or if they are okay that the world still has its misgivings about them. We are taught to see them as somehow inferior, and to measure them by the standards of heterosexual lives, which are held up as the ideal. When we are young we believe what we hear. This is how the psyche works, especially in girls who can be very sensitive to their surroundings. When we busy ourselves scanning the faces of those around us, interpreting their reactions and vocal cues to understand our place in the world, we believe what the world shows us.

Eventually, the messages become intolerable. Because they are so painful and self-erasing, we don't want to let ourselves feel them, and soon we start to bury them deep within the recesses of our unconscious. This is especially harmful for girls who have no one to teach them otherwise, no one to counter the demeaning messages, or replace them with lesbian-affirmative or diversity-affirmative messages. In the absence of a role model who can help us edit and reinterpret the homophobic content we absorb in our daily lives, someone who shows us that these messages are wrong, they go into our psyches, where they are stored away for future work. Most girls grow up without ever hearing how wonderful it is to be a lesbian. Even those in tolerant households have found that lesbians are usually invisible. Sadly, far too many lesbians grow up surrounded by intolerant and hateful attitudes toward same-sex love and relationships. Things are slowly getting better, and lesbian representation is gradually increasing in the media. More recent television shows such as *The Fosters*, in which a lesbian couple raise a family, seem to indicate a shift in the general attitude toward same-sex parenting. However, for the most part, popular culture remains heterosexually focused, and lesbians are still absent from the media. Do you remember the last time you saw a lesbian in a children's story or a fairytale?[7] Neither do I.

In chapter 2, we looked briefly at what starts to happen during adolescence when our sex hormones kick in. For most girls, this is when the internal critic comes into our lives—and makes itself at home. As this happens, we can become greatly self-conscious about our physical selves or criticize every part of our body, our gender expression, or our overall capabilities. This can also manifest in our finding fault in others. When the internal critic is suppressed, we turn our attention to others, finding everything wrong or unworthy in others because it is easier than looking at our own limitations. This is common for all of us at some point in our lives. Fault and focusing blame on the people around us distracts us from the often intolerable feelings that surface in adolescence. The problem is that being hypercritical about yourself or about others doesn't get to the heart of the problem, which is the negative messages that are difficult to filter out. As young women we are bombarded by news and information that dictate the rules of femininity and of sexuality. Left unquestioned and treated as facts, we are at risk of experiencing them as truths.

Adolescence is a difficult time. With a sea change taking place in our bodies and our minds, suddenly we are experiencing and feeling things in a completely new way as our hormones take control and our worldview begins to widen. For those of us who realized that they were attracted to women during this time, the complexity of adolescence doubled. Knowing that our families and our culture expect us to celebrate and embrace heterosexuality leads to confusion, internalized anger or shame, and the feeling that we should not be true to ourselves. These powerful feelings can be overwhelming, and for many relief comes in the form of drinking and drugs. Unfortunately, all of this creates the perfect opening for love addiction behavior, which can start just as we're beginning to figure things out.

HOMOPHOBIA VERSUS LESBIANPHOBIA

When I work with my lesbian clients who are dealing with lesbian love addiction (whether they know it or not—and they usually don't during their first visit), we often begin by recalling and naming specific traumas. As painful as it can be to revisit buried feelings, it is a very effective way to start the healing process. To describe what I see as lesbian-specific trauma, I have coined the word *lesbianphobia*. It's probably not a term you have heard many times before. I developed it after years of working in the LGBTQ community, where I would hear the word *homophobia* used to describe both gay men and lesbians. The problem is, the word *homophobia* doesn't incorporate our unique lesbian issues in the same way that *gay* does not describe a woman's love for other women. The word *lesbian* was embraced by the lesbian community in the early 1970s to respond to that lack and to redress the term *gay*, which many women felt was too male-centric (as many gay-centric ideas are), and I felt a similar lack in our understanding of homophobia.

I began to use the word *lesbianphobia* to separate out the very specific traumas to which lesbian women are subjected. While we share some of the same traumas, our experiences and struggles are very different from those experienced by gay men. With lesbianphobia, we have a word that helps us understand exactly what we are dealing with, which is a good first step on the journey to healing.

What Is Homophobia?

Before we explore lesbianphobia, I think this is a good time to talk a bit more about homophobia. As most of you already know, homophobia is the irrational fear or hatred of homosexuals and homosexual behavior, a horribly prejudicial and harmful belief system that is rampant around the world.[8] Homophobia comes from the societal and familial conditioning that is called heterocentrism. As seen in the diagram in figure 3-1, heterosexism develops out of heterocentrism. Heterosexism is the system that enforces the heterocentric ideals.[9]

Adrienne Rich expanded on the idea of heteronormity by emphasizing that heterosexuality is *compulsory*—meaning it is what is expected of all people[10] and those who are not heterosexual have unique environmental and personal challenges that influence their identity development and socialization processes.[11] The expectation that all humans are innately heterosexual greatly influences the way we feel about ourselves, most egregiously when we realize we are not fulfilling that expectation for others, especially our families. These thoughts are usually quite unconscious, until we have to face coming out, and even then it can be pushed back into our unconscious because the idea of defying the system can be so terrifying.[12]

Heterocentrism is a learned concept, created by a culture fearful of difference and deviation from the status quo. The strongest and often most vocal objectors are people whose fear goes so deep that their homophobia embraces hatred. Most of us have experienced feelings of hatred at some point. Hate is a common human emotion. When a feeling of hatred is projected onto a group of people simply because they are different, it is called prejudice. Anything or anyone who is perceived as a threat to a belief system can be the target of prejudice. We see it all the time through the United States' ongoing endemic problem with racism. Some people find comfort in hating the people

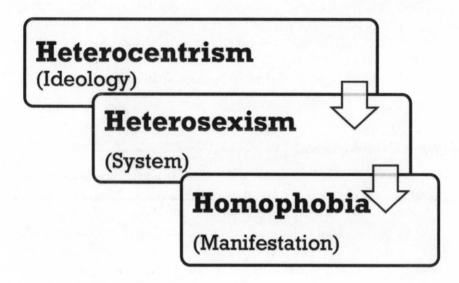

who belong to a group other than their own. In this way, prejudice
allows them to avoid looking at their own unhappiness and imperfect
nature by turning their critical focus onto others. Perhaps dumping
their pain onto others provides temporary relief from the pain that
hatred and fear brings up in them. This is called scapegoating.[13]

Those who live and think outside of the heterocentric view of the
world might also become a convenient distraction for people trying to
avoid looking into their own shadows, a concept I briefly describe in
chapter 2. If you find a group to hate, you don't have to look critically at
your own problems and inadequacies, or see how your destructive
mindset affects your own relationships and your own potential. Homophobia can also hide latent feelings of same-sex attraction that are much
too frightening for the homophobic person to face. Hamlet's observa-
tions, "The lady doth protest too much, methinks," which implies the
lady has a guilty conscience, may also apply to those who protest too
much about "the homosexuals" and is something to keep in mind whenever you encounter homophobic hate speech.[14]

Lesbianphobia

Institutionalized lesbianphobia is therefore the fear or hatred of lesbians due to the systemic promotion and cultivation of both misogyny and homophobia.[15] Lesbianphobia is a women-centric concept, one that highlights the lesbian experience and puts the unique issues shared by lesbians front and center. Lesbians exist in a world that is both male privileged and homophobic. Lesbianphobia embodies the knowledge that lesbians are deeply affected by heterosexual privilege and harmed by both the homophobic and misogynistic belief systems that dominate the world we live in.

CHARACTERISTICS OF HETEROCENTRIC AND LESBIANPHOBIC THINKING

Recognizing heterocentrism and lesbianphobia in action becomes more obvious if you know what you are looking for. These are some of the characteristics and behaviors that might help you to identify people who are heterocentric and lesbianphobic in their thinking.[16]

- Being from an older, less tolerant generation
- Holding misogynistic and sexist points of view
- Identifying with or belonging to a conservative religion
- Seeing lesbians only through the lens of sexual behavior
- Being less open-minded and permissive about sexuality in general
- Having little to no exposure to people from the LGBTQ community
- Refusing to learn about anything or anyone unlike oneself
- Expressing high levels of authoritarianism
- Being prone to rigid thinking in general

This list could describe the thoughts and behaviors of your parents, your grandparents, your siblings, or the town or state or culture you grew up in. Homophobia and lesbianphobia are pervasive, but similar to the way that racism continues to live silently inside of many people, the practice of hiding one's intolerance can ensure that it will survive and never be questioned or threatened. Many people guard their prejudice securely, knowing that if they expose it they risk having to change their opinions.

Lesbianphobia originates from our difference—being women and same-sex oriented—and the way that society and the people around us react to and feel about this difference. The first and obvious form of lesbianphobia is the fear and judgment that comes from others. This type of lesbianphobia is relatively easy to recognize. However, our internal psychological responses are more complicated. The psychological response to intolerance often emerges in generalized feelings of anger and fury about the outside world. But there is another more insidious primal emotion, what spiritual counselor and author John Bradshaw calls *toxic shame*. [17] When strong feelings of shame take over, they stimulate the SNS and our fight-or-flight response. People who experience toxic shame feel exposed and want to hide. Sometimes they react with rage.

As you can imagine, toxic shame is a painful and troubling reaction to primal shame. Lesbianphobia that creates toxic shame is also responsible for institutional discrimination. For thousands of years our way of being in the world has been hated and rejected, and that disdain has been deeply ingrained in our culture. We experience institutional lesbianphobia in the many large and small acts we encounter in the course of our daily lives, when we are not understood or included—when we are invisible. In many areas of the world, lesbians have to hide their true selves. They are glared at and subject to cruel, ignorant, judgmental, and hurtful comments. The Showtime documentary about lesbians living in the conservative Deep South, *The L Word Mississippi: Hate the Sin*, illustrates the treatment that many lesbians endure in places where people are often passionately lesbianphobic. [18] Unfortunately, far too many women know just how difficult it can be to be a lesbian in a geographical area that is this hostile to same-sex love.

In reality, none of us are exempt from the effects of lesbianphobia no matter where we live. While this is slowly changing with shows like *Transparent* and *Orange Is the New Black*, every time, for the most part, when we walk outside and engage with our neighbors and coworkers, every time we watch TV or look at magazines, we are barraged by heteronormative missives. They come in all forms, from the heterosexually oriented paperwork at our doctor's office, to the travel plans and hotel accommodations that are made with the assumption that our partner must be a husband and not a wife or girlfriend. The television commercials and shows that focus primarily on straight folks and heterosexual families, the movies that place heterosexual relationships at the center of our attention, all of this contributes greatly to the public's understanding of human sexuality. Since lesbians have been excluded from popular culture, left out of public discourse, and over-shadowed by heteronormativity for thousands of years, we have been wiped from our cultural consciousness. Becoming mindful of how this invisibility and lack of inclusion impacts the way you feel about yourself is an important part of lesbian-affirmative inner work.

A LESBIAN SENSE OF SELF

Growing up in a heterocentric and lesbianphobic society can have a tremendous effect on our mental health. And we are not alone in this. In many ways, these phobic attitudes and rigidly defined rules affect everyone's mental health because they don't accept and normalize the full human spectrum of sexuality that is present in each of us.[19] The American Jewish poet and activist, Emma Lazarus (1849–1887), said it the best, "Until we are all free, none of us are free."[20] Her words highlight the idea that even with these incredibly changing times and more straight folks becoming allies, there is still much to be done for all LGBTQ people to be free from heterocentrism and LGBTQ phobias. Because we are not there yet, lesbians are still at risk for mental and physical health problems caused by lesbianphobia and toxic shame. When we internalize these lesbianphobic messages and absorb discrim-ination daily, we suffer emotionally and physically. In lesbian-affirma-tive psychotherapy we call this internalized lesbianphobia. It may not surprise you to learn how often internalized lesbianphobia lands a star-ring role in love addiction.[21]

Internalized Lesbianphobia

Heterosexism is often enforced by intimidation, harassment, and the silencing that is the result of exclusion and invisibility. The people who make up the LGBTQ community are some of the most distressed indi-viduals in our society.[22] Our difference alone can make us targets of

hatred and violence.[23] Internalized lesbianphobia is the unhealthy outcome from a lifetime of conditioning that happened long before our
equality movement got momentum. We are all vulnerable to the same
false belief systems that limit our understanding of sexuality, especially
those that originate during childhood and develop unconsciously as we
become adults.

In lesbian-affirmative psychotherapy, we recognize these false belief
systems as trauma to the developing self, and treat it as a very real
threat to our mental and emotional well-being. Seeing it clearly as trauma helps us to recognize the weight it has carried in our minds and can
empower us to stand up and confront it as such. Because the internalization of heterocentric messages is the real source of the problem, we
recognize that lesbian-specific psychological problems are the result. As
lesbians, we are not responsible for creating a lesbianphobic and
heterosexist culture that negates us, nor should we blame ourselves for
the influence it has on our mental health and addiction issues. Internalized lesbianphobia, therefore, is not a pathology (or disease) within the
lesbian herself, but an internalization of the psychologically harmful
ideologies that the lesbian has absorbed throughout her life. Prejudice
and intolerance have always been unhealthy, and throughout history
humans have suffered greatly from their power. Recognizing the multi-
tude of ways to love and be in the world,[24] the continuum of human
sexuality goes a long way toward creating healthy, well-adjusted people.
Unfortunately, embracing the true dimensions of sexuality scares people who are rigid in their thinking. Those who live at odds with their
own differences often find it easier to dismiss the people who represent
difference rather than contend with their own fear.

The Impact of the Phobias

Because of our deeply flawed systems, many lesbians come to believe
that something is inherently wrong with them. The impact that this
well-hidden belief has on our self-worth bears a close and critical exam-
ination. Once we recognize the many difficult feelings that surface as a
result of this false thinking, we can begin to heal. Believing that we are
not right or that we don't fit in, many lesbians and women in general
carry with them a persistent need to belong. This can lead to self-

hatred, perfectionism, and an overarching fear of confronting our true feelings, all of which tax our mental and emotional well-being.

With these unhealthy belief systems, vulnerability to addiction increases, and many lesbians find themselves turning to drugs and alcohol to blunt the pain they have buried inside. Love addiction is often a lesbian's drug of choice, because on the surface it may not look like a drug at all. This is why awareness is key, the first and often most effective step to preventing love addiction. In my work as a therapist, one of the most rewarding feats I can do is to help lesbians uncover their internalized lesbianphobia and begin the rewarding process of deposing its power. It's truly beautiful to witness.

When Carla, a thirty-something Latina femme lesbian, started working with me, she was challenged by the idea of internalized lesbianphobia. Culturally, she had been taught not to question the elders of her community or dispute their view of the world. Despite being out to her parents, she felt a lot of shame about being a lesbian. Like many families, Carla's employed the "don't ask, don't tell" rule,[25] and so her sexuality was an issue that her family avoided altogether. As long as Carla didn't mention it, or introduce her family to any of the women she dated or hung out with, everyone was fine with who she was. Carla played into this invisibility game, and this left her feeling guilty about her position in the family. She saw her lesbianism as a burden she was inflicting upon her family. In therapy, we touched on the idea of lesbianphobia, while being culturally sensitive to her relatives that were from the old country. It was important for Carla to understand how lesbianphobia had harmed her and made her shy away from women she encountered. Over many sessions we delved into the ways her family and the world's lesbianphobia affected her self-esteem and how that compromised her ability to create a long-lasting relationship with a woman without demonizing her family or ruining her relationship with them.

What Makes Us Who We Are

In light of these issues that affect all lesbians, regardless of status or geographic location, it might be useful for me to reiterate the fundamental components of our psychological makeup. Our sense of self is essentially an accumulation of all we've experienced, the personal stories we've lived, interpreted, rewritten, revised, and internalized. To live is to continually review and make sense of our human experiences. We become grounded and secure through the awareness of who we are, and this awareness allows us to live authentically.

The psychologist's job is to help us interpret our stories and guide us in better understanding our experiences, which shape our identity and our sense of self. Psychologists look closely at development, starting with when we're born, and create theories and concepts and evidence-based treatment protocols to explain how the psyche and our mental processes work. By creating a vocabulary we can use to understand our development, psychology itself builds and revises a universe of helpful theories and guidelines that are meant to open up and uncover truths about the human experience. The first step on our journey to understanding love addiction via the lesbian psyche must be to explore these building blocks.

Mapping the Self

There is a general roadmap many psychologists use for understanding some of the major components of mental health and our sense of self. I find it to be one of the most intriguing of all our Western ideas of what it means to be human and alive and healthy. This roadmap highlights the many concepts of human dynamics that psychologists and psychotherapists have in mind when seeing clients. I want to explain them here so that you too can understand this map and see yourself in it—so that you can really begin to understand what a positive sense of self really means.

As you discovered in the chapter exploring the female brain, our fundamental ways of relating begin in utero and continue into our mid-teenage years. Psychology considers this time to be crucial and uses it to explain how we flourish in our families and in society. Contained in these years are the experiences that represent how we felt loved, nurtured, and understood, as well as the ways in which we may have been neglected, unseen, or made to feel fragmented. As discussed in the chapter on how we connect, those who grow up with less inner conflict, less doubt about their parent's love and their own self-worth, those who felt protected and held, find it easier to thrive and feel joy as adults. This secure attachment makes it more likely for us to initiate and maintain healthy and loving relationships. When we grow up feeling loved and insulated from harm with parents who accept us, even with our complicated feelings, our anger, hurt, aggression, jealousy, envy, and selfishness, which are part of being human, we are more tolerant of our difficult feelings, primarily because we don't feel as much shame for having them. Granted, with the ability to accept the totality of who we are we develop a strong sense of self. With that strong sense of self, it is much easier to live authentically, to know and believe we are lovable, and to make our world a safe place.

In the absence of growing up feeling safe and loved, our psyches become vulnerable and fragile, and we develop insecure attachment patterns. We become unsure of ourselves and less than confident in our abilities. When we don't believe in ourselves, it is much harder to be productive and to thrive as adults because our inner critic runs the show.[26] Of course, as deeply resilient women, we also possess many strengths, those parts that make up the confident, proud, caring, fun, smart, successful lesbian that you are. Our resilience and intelligence give us the ability to be strong despite the internal trauma we've experienced.[27] This invincible nature is an integral part of the lesbian spirit, which we carry inside. Regardless of the hostile world we grow up in, and the pressure we face to be heterosexual, most of us find the strength to come out, an amazing feat in itself. We grow up, find careers, often develop strong lesbian families of choice, and sometimes have families of our own. We do this although we did not feel understood and safe as children.

The Word *Lesbian* and the Lesbian Sense of Self

I have found through my work in the lesbian community that many of us don't even know where or how the word *lesbian* originated. I have also discovered that many lesbians prefer to call themselves *gay women* instead of lesbians. There is an important difference between the terms *gay woman* and *lesbian*, which I believe can affect our self-esteem. We will examine the reasons for this later in this chapter, but for now let's look at the history of this word that some people find difficult to utter.

Lesbian originates from Lesbos, a Greek island that was the homeland of Sappho, who was born around 630 BCE and lived and taught until she died in 570 BCE. Sappho is not only a lesbian icon, she is one of the most important women in Western history—not an easy feat in a world that historically records only men's accomplishments. She was one of the most influential poets of Western civilization—her style is still revered today. As a poet she wrote passionately about the joy and agony of her love for other women. The word *Lesbian* was coined from the island from which she came, Lesbos. This was chosen out of the connection lesbians from the early gay liberation movement had to her work. So, if you think about it, one of the most important poets of Western civilization was a woman who loved women![28] Although our history has been based on a patriarchal and heteronormative point of view, and much of our civilization has been male dominated, one of our lesbian sisters was the first to express love, depth, and meaning through the written word about women who love women. It isn't hard to imagine why one of the most important poetess of love was a lesbian if we consider the intensity with which lesbians love. You can probably detect my enormous respect for Sappho, whose name has survived thousands of years of desecration and heterocentric propaganda. And even with the many attempts to annihilate her enormous contribution to Western civilization, Sappho remains, even today, the honored Lesbian archetype and powerful symbol of the sacred for all women.

If you have trouble with the word *lesbian*, you are not alone. My hope is that in knowing the word's history, you will come to appreciate and respect what it symbolizes and why it is significant for us to embrace. If I can provide a deeper context to the issues lesbians face growing up in a heterocentric and lesbianphobic world, then I know I have done some good. Above all else, what is truly important is the step you've taken in choosing to read this book. That alone is courageous, and it is your courage that will take you far.

To refer to ourselves as *lesbian* instead of *gay* is to proudly declare our inherent distinction. *Gay* is largely a male-centric term, one that was coined by gay men, and it did not have much to do with lesbian love or identity. To say *lesbian* is to clarify that while we may have in common same-sex love, we are not gay men. For the development of a healthy sense of self, we locate our uniqueness and award it the special attention and love it needs and deserves. For each of us to heal and embrace our authentic selves, distinguishing ourselves through our identity is an important and helpful step.

GENDER EXPRESSION

Another way to think about a lesbian sense of self is to consider the range of lesbian gender expressions from butch to femme (and all those in between, which I like to call "tweeners"). This range of gender expressions makes us and our lesbian community unique. We tend to fashion ourselves outside the more rigid heterosexist gender roles. Pushing others to think outside the gender box has been a role that LGBTQ people have been playing for thousands of years, and in every part of the world.[29] Unfortunately, as I mentioned earlier, variant gender expressions can also be distressing for those who embody them.

One of the most discriminated groups in the lesbian communities has been butch, boi, or masculine-identified lesbians. They are the lesbian women who embody a beautiful masculine energy and feel more comfortable in traditional men's style clothing and short hair. Butch lesbians have suffered historically and were brutally raped and beaten during the 1940s to the 1970s when police raided lesbian bars.[30] Today, butch lesbians still experience discrimination and shaming attitudes from other women, such as being treated with hostility for simply using the women's restroom. As young girls, butch lesbians are often tomboys—in childhood or early adolescence it is more culturally acceptable for girls to be boyish. Once puberty hits, however, society demands that all girls embody a traditional concept of femininity. It dictates that girls measure themselves and their worth by the degree to which they are attractive to men, and it defines the rules of attractiveness by conventional—and narrow—standards of femininity. Girls who do not fit nicely into these prescribed roles face even more pressure from other girls, especially from those friends who are more invested in following the rules.

After puberty, there is very little room left for tomboys, or butch/boi lesbians in our culture. Many lesbians who assimilate their gender-expression by trying to conform to familial and societal standards do so with great discomfort. It can be doubly difficult to come out as lesbian and as butch, but doing so is critical to the self-acceptance process. Prioritizing her own needs, above offering comfort to her family, is a courageous task for any young woman, and it deserves recognition.

Femme lesbians experience a different kind of societal response that is nonetheless replete with discrimination. On the basis of their physical characteristics, femmes are often pushed to be straight by family members who have no regard for their authenticity or knowledge that lesbians come in all shapes and sizes and styles. Femme lesbians are also approached more often by men, and because most heterosexuals may assume they are straight, they have to repeatedly restate their sexual orientation in social situations or pretend to be straight but unavailable, which, depending on her level of lesbianphobia, can go from feeling slightly uncomfortable to downright scary.

Lesbians experience a great deal in their day-to-day lives that heterosexual people don't experience. We live with so many extra responses to our being, of which most people are unaware. Yet there is good that comes from this. As much as these discriminating experiences have the power to harden us, they also make us stronger people. Historically, lesbians have been at the grassroots level of some of the most important social justice movements, including the abolitionist movement, the suffragist movement, and many iterations and generations of the feminist movement. We have learned how to deal with public ignorance and thrive in spite of it all—and this creates resilience and strength that is life affirming.

Chuck and her wife, a butch femme, an Asian American couple, came to see me for premarital counseling. They just wanted to check to make sure their relationship was on the right track. After several sessions, it was obvious this couple was deeply in love and great for each other. Over the years of being together, they had figured out how to settle misunderstandings or disputes. When something did trigger them they would take a little time away from each other to sit with their feelings. This helped keep them from projecting or demonizing the other. They would also figure out, before taking the break, what length of time they would need before they should come back together and talk. This depended on the strength of the traumas each of them was experiencing. They had also realized that if they needed more time to sort through their stories and feelings they would acknowledge to the other that they needed a bit more time to process, but would be connecting soon. This had become a recipe for much success.

As many of you may know, there is a great challenge involved in becoming psychologically stronger. Through our resilience, we are also affected by the things that eventually undermine our strength, which we will explore shortly. The bottom line is, our internalized lesbianphobia affects us all—the proud and out, as well as those who are still in the closet about their sexuality. Overburdened by a heterosexist culture that minimizes our worth, many lesbians find a remedy for their struggles through love addiction. Initially, this love we experience so intensely quickly makes us feel better. Our relationships, while unhealthy, make us feel safe and secure in this often hostile world. Our brains signal us and guide us toward relationships because ultimately these connections are good for us. That is, unless you are a love addict, in which case your ability to pick a healthy partner or create a healthy relationship is impaired.

LESBIAN VISIBILITY AND INVISIBILITY

As mentioned earlier, media visibility for lesbians is increasing in the United States because of programs such as *Orange Is the New Black*, *The Real L Word*, *The L Word* series, *The Fosters*, and, of course, the groundbreaking episode of *The Ellen Show* in 1997,[31] when Ellen came out to the nation. While these cultural developments are critical, it does not override how past invisiblity in popular culture has negatively affected us. The absence of role models in our chronicallly heterocentric world is a contributing factor to internalized lesbianphobia.

Lesbians rarely see themselves represented in everyday life, and consequently the opportunity to feel and to be seen as important and valuable is missed. Psychologically speaking, this creates an internal struggle. It is difficult to develop authentic self-love when our culture, family, community, and media overlook or pretend we don't exist. It is this lack of validation and failure of inclusion that creates the sense of not belonging. If we are told that we don't matter, then how can we believe in ourselves? These are some of the uncertainties and the self-worth struggles that lie at the heart of love addiction.

Why Is This Important?

Not surprisingly, studies reveal that lesbians have higher rates of addictive disorders than their heterosexual counterparts.[32] Higher rates of substance abuse are also linked to internalized phobias. Research has shown that substance use is correlated with the desire to mask feelings of self-hatred.[33] It is not a stretch, then, to consider that love addiction can be linked in similar ways.

In this next chapter, we will look more closely at the different kinds of lesbian love addiction. As we move through the chapter, my hope is you'll begin to see how our brains, which are wired to love, can suffer trauma when a faulty attachment occurs and a hostile world follows. I know that this material is not the easiest to sit with, but I assure you that things will brighten as we move past the problems and into ways to heal, which will be examined in chapter 6. Before we get there, let's look at some more helpful information.

4

HOW WE MERGE AND SPIRAL

I made you and take you made into me.

—Audrey Lorde[1]

Hopefully you have a little more insight into how and why a lesbian can become a love addict. This comes from understanding how our brains are wired, how those feel-good chemicals and hormones influence our behavior, and the effect that attachment issues and heterocentric and lesbianphobic trauma can have on our sense of self and feelings of self-worth. As lesbians, our ability to hold on to our authenticity and maintain a healthy relationship with ourselves first, and with others second, is critical for self-care and self-love. Now let's look at what lesbian love addiction actually is.

LESBIAN LOVE ADDICTION

While love addiction is not yet recognized by the *Diagnostic and Statistical Manual of Mental Disorders*, fifth edition (DSM-5),[2] criteria to identify addiction as a whole has been established by the American Psychiatric Association[3] and scientific organizations including the American Society of Addiction Medicine (ASAM).[4] Since love addiction does not involve the ingestion of a specific substance, professionals often refer to it as a *process addiction*. This means it is an addiction based mostly on behaviors.[5] Because these behaviors do not require complete abstinence to stay well, the addiction itself is to the *process* or function the lesbian uses to cope with her feelings or trauma. But let's look at addiction first. The following is the criteria often used by mental health professionals when diagnosing addictions.

Criteria for Addiction

- Obsession of the addiction or behavior
- Cravings for more of the addiction
- Tolerance or need for more of the addiction or behavior to obtain desired effect
- Denial of any problem
- Diminished capacity to control one's behavior while in the addiction
- Negative impact on interpersonal relationships
- Inability to stop using despite repeated attempts to quit on one's own
- Withdrawal when the addiction or behaviors are taken away

Love addiction has been referred to as an addiction—with real physical and psychological components—by psychologists and theorists for decades. How it fits with other characteristics of addiction is described well in an article about rejection by Dr. Fisher and her colleagues called "Reward, Addiction, and Emotion Regulation Systems Associated with Rejection in Love":

> Several psychologists regard romantic love as an addiction because it shows addiction characteristics such as the lover's intensely focused attention on a preferred individual, mood swings, craving, obsession, compulsion, distortion of reality, emotional dependence, personality changes, risk-taking, and loss of self-control.[6]

Keep these criteria in mind as we start to cover in detail the particular hallmarks of lesbian love addiction.

Love addiction manifests in a variety of ways; therefore, it is important to know how to identify the culprit as it appears. This means knowing exactly what shape it can take and how the experience varies from woman to woman. Some lesbians become addicted to a particular woman and find themselves unable to draw psychological or physical boundaries. Most often lesbians fall into one of two love addiction categories while others have characteristics of both, depending on the relationship, in what Pia Mellody calls in her book *Facing Love Addiction* love addicts and love avoidants.[7] Lesbians love addicts find it extremely painful to be without a partner and look for love at any cost. Lesbians who are avoidant get off on the initial high of attraction or the power of seduction, but they frequently leave the relationship once the chase is over—literally, mentally, or energetically. No matter how love addiction behavior plays out, at its core is the same fundamental problem: an intimacy disorder. What love addicts and love avoidants have in common is a false sense of intimacy. Unfortunately for each of these types, healthy and authentic intimacy—which can hold the good, the bad, and everything in between—is eclipsed by the past traumas these women have experienced. The *urge to merge* is so powerful that the reality of what creates and sustains real intimacy is lost, or overridden by the fantasy of love. Infatuated with the merge and all that it promises to deliver, love addicts dive head first into a relationship with each other to satisfy their cravings. Merging is such a common pattern for lesbian love-addicted relationships that it inspired the subtitle of this book.

The Addict and the Avoidant

What makes love addiction even more interesting—and complicated— is that love addicts and love avoidants are drawn to each other and are often in relationships together. Since this is relationship dependent, you may have found yourself embodying both styles in your relationship history. You may lean in one direction most of the time such as being mostly a love addict, but remember being love avoidant with certain types of women. We saw this with Mary, Charley, and Matilda. While no evidence-based research explains this phenomenon yet, psychologically speaking, it makes sense. Two people struggling with an intimacy disorder will play the two styles out depending on the dynamic between them. One question to ponder: Are love addicts love avoidants attracted to each other, or the familiar drama that is about to unfold? You could say the love addict and the love avoidant styles are two moths drawn to the same flame. Their addiction may manifest in opposite ways, but the urge to merge burns brightly, like a flare blazing in the darkness. We'll explore this phenomenon in greater detail a bit later.

For now, let's focus on all the characteristics of the love addict and love avoidant, how they can become quickly enmeshed, and how this entanglement relates to everything else we've learned.

Several books on the subject of addiction have been instrumental in my practice. *Facing Love Addiction: Giving Yourself the Power to Change the Way You Love* by Pia Mellody, *Ready to Heal: Breaking Free of Addictive Relationships* by Kelly McDaniel, and *How to Break Your Addiction to a Person* by Howard Halpern are all pioneering works that examine unhealthy and obsessive behaviors in love and relationships and how to heal from the destructive patterns that define love addiction.

But love addiction has rarely, if ever, been thoroughly explored from a lesbian-affirmative perspective. Without this perspective, lesbians lose out on valuable information that would help them break the pattern of unsustainable and often injurious relationships. By continuing on with the stories you have been following so far—Mary, Jane, Matilda, Charley, Chuck, Janya, Carla, and you'll meet Josie—I hope to illuminate the unique love addiction issues that lesbians face. It is my hope that you'll see some of your own experiences as you read through the personal stories that I've gathered here. Paying attention to what jumps out at you, and what you can relate to, might help start your own healing process. Awareness is the first step to making any change.

CHARACTERISTICS OF A LOVE ADDICT

Let's look more closely at the unique characteristics the lesbian love addict style shares.

The Urge to Merge

Lesbian love addicts idealize the woman they fall in love with and often assign her magical qualities. She sees her object of affection as perfect in every way. Once the infatuation with her begins, a love addict becomes preoccupied and spends an inordinate amount of time thinking about her and longing to be with her. This "falling in love" process creates a physical high as the sexual attraction and romantic feelings begin and the brain releases large amounts of dopamine and oxytocin.

Thoughts of being together forever are extremely common. The physical high drives an intense desire to merge with the woman whom she barely knows. As the actual merging takes place, the continual release of dopamine and oxytocin that the women experience during physical and emotional connection increases. This *oxytocin fest*, if you will, feels amazing for both women, and as these potent feelings intensify, they are mistaken for true intimacy.

Intensity Mistaken for Intimacy

The mirage of closeness that the couple creates is deceptive and misleading. Nevertheless, many lesbians find it extremely addictive, but no one more so than the love addict. The initial intense feelings the lesbian feels for her new love interest gives her a false sense of intimacy. The sex is often as intense as the intimacy feels. While the merging certainly feels intimate, the reality is that the love addict does not yet know the woman she is falling in love with. The merging quality, the hard-wired ability to connect, the oxytocin and dopamine, combined with attachment issues create a dangerous delusion of authentic intimacy. Believing she can trust this woman she has just met, she lets down her guard, becomes too vulnerable too fast, and jumps into a committed relationship too quickly.

Oh, the Drama

Another sure-fire way to recognize lesbian love addict relationships is by their dramatic features. The crazy, sometimes manic behavior generated by the two as they are falling in love, the frequent fighting, the breakups, the secretive affairs, the abrupt abandonment, and the stalking behaviors these women engage in when they feel desperate and "dumped," without explanation, all take an incredible emotional toll on the psyche. Lori Jean Glass from Five Sisters Ranch, a women's love addiction treatment center in Northern California, lovingly coins this behavior "Riding the Crazy Train," which she addresses in the love addiction seminars she developed.[8] Something that all addictions share is the unconscious behavior that drives the addict. No woman wants to see herself behave erratically or recklessly, but lacking insight about her motivations and feeling controlled by her emotional wounds, she unconsciously acts out desperate or dramatic behavior that is proportional to the trauma and craziness she feels inside. In short, the addict becomes preoccupied with the object of her addiction because of the intensity the connection with her brings. These unconscious patterns are familiar methods of achieving these heightened feelings. Denial is also hard at work. It is important to remember that the problems the lesbian love addict encounters in her most intimate relationship derive from the addiction, and not the woman she desires.

Mary and Tina's back-and-forth relationship greatly illustrates the drama possible in a lesbian love-addicted relationship. Tina broke up with Mary so many times that Mary lost count. Every time Tina returned, it was with dramatic urgency, dropping everything and running over to see Mary or rushing in to rescue Mary whenever she had even a minor problem. The two women played it big, ripping each other's clothes off, and proclaiming undying love for each other time and time again. The breakups would be just as dramatic—fights in public, disastrous and theatrical sexual experiences, screaming matches over the phone. Their dynamic was very black and white. Either they were going to spend the rest of their lives marinating in the blissful blend of dopamine and oxytocin their bodies produced together, or they were breaking up. Eventually, these patterns left Mary so hurt and enraged that she had to cut Tina out of her life completely.

Boundaries—What Are Those?

Lesbian love addicts have difficulty setting boundaries and holding on to a strong sense of self. They trust too quickly and become vulnerable without maintaining healthy boundaries. They pursue and get deeply involved with women before knowing who they are or if they are compatible, which often leads to destructive situations and broken hearts that create unfathomable emotional pain.

Dissatisfied with her partner of ten years but emotionally unable to leave, Charley asserted her will unconsciously by actively flirting with other women. Since she initially never engaged sexually with any of them, she did not see her habitual flirting as a problem, nor did she think she was breaking her vows. She rationalized her behavior by blaming it on her sexless marriage. Little did Charley know that one of her key struggles was, and had always been, with emotional boundaries.

Her family did not maintain healthy boundaries. The man who abused her certainly never respected any of her boundaries, and that experience had robbed Charley of her self-respect and a sense of control. Her marriage was deeply satisfying in the beginning, as many lesbian relationships are, but once the romance waned, sex became virtually nonexistent. Feeling hurt and abandoned by her wife's loss of interest, she fed her love addiction by seducing other women. Instead of taking care of herself and seeking help, Charley played out her feelings with strangers. Doing this gave Charley a sense of power and confidence she did not experience in other areas of her life, especially with her wife.

Fear of Abandonment

An uncontrollable fear of abandonment makes a lesbian love addict especially sensitive to her partner's need for autonomy. Addicted to the honeymoon period and the feel-good chemicals released into her system during the merge, any shift away from it triggers abandonment issues. When the merging stops, the love addict experiences withdrawal from the dopamine and oxytocin, which in turn causes more panic. At the same time, the shift in attention and connection withdrawal triggers her childhood attachment issues and her core fear of abandonment. This absence makes her feel out of control, and now that she is swimming in her anxiety, she becomes more needy and clingy.

But You Said You Would Love Me No Matter What!

Unfortunately, unresolved attachment issues, childhood trauma, heterosexist bias, and internalized lesbianphobia can lead lesbian love addicts to have unrealistic expectations for relationships. In *Facing Love Addiction*, Pia Mellody uses the term *unconditional positive regard* (UPR), coined by pioneering psychologist Carl Rogers in the 1960s[9] to characterize the unrealistic emotional requirements that love addicts demand from their partners. Used in therapy, UPR can be a great tool to help heal the client who did not receive enough positive regard from her parents. However, it is untenable in a romantic relationship. Needing unconditional positive regard to feel loved not only creates a fragile connection, it places all the responsibility on the addict's partner who must unconditionally soothe the addict's every discomfort, always agreeing with her, predicting her needs and thoughts and, if she wants to avoid a conflict, becoming skilled at reading her mind.

As you can imagine, no partner can fulfill these needs, and asking a person to do so is not only unfair, it places greatly unrealistic expectations and pressure on a relationship and leads inevitably to chronic disappointment. Once the pleasure associated with merging dissipates, a void of emptiness remains. This is when trauma from the broken attachment with one's mother gets activated, creating more anxiety and discontent.

In the beginning of their relationship, Mary and Jane seemed to agree on everything. This helped to contribute to their quick bond. The similarities felt liberating. Over time though, Mary started to notice that Jane was backtracking on things the two used to agree on. Mary found these minor differences intolerable to her sense of self. These small gestures of independence felt like personal jabs to Mary. They put her into a defensive mode and disrupted the comfort she experienced being in a relationship, and her high from merging. When she and Jane had behaved as one person, Mary felt composed and connected, but once Jane started to show interests that were different from her own, Mary's fears resurfaced. Soon she was overwhelmed by powerful and confusing feelings. She thought of herself as a supportive partner and wanted to demonstrate that to Jane, but because Mary was addicted to falling in love, she began to worry that Jane was not a good match for her after all. This left her feeling anxious and uneasy about the future.

What Is Self-Care?

Fueled by her fear of abandonment or an all-consuming desire to find Ms. Right, the lesbian love addict often stops caring for herself—emotionally, physically, and even financially. She might lose touch with friends, neglect her family, and jeopardize her career in an effort to find a partner, please her partner, and keep the merging going. In hot pursuit of her next love, she compromises her own sense of self by valuing romantic connection over a balanced life. She may have no idea what lies beneath her anxiety, and because her behavior is motivated by fear that is largely unconscious, she won't recognize the problem until she sees that these patterns are repeated with each new lover. She may begin to notice that the sacrifices she makes for her lovers are rarely ever reciprocated, but the insight stops there. This is often when depression and hopelessness set in, and feeling down makes it more difficult for her to figure out what or how to change.

Matilda came out when she was sixteen. Around that time she came to see me. Thankfully, Matilda's mother was very supportive, and this emboldened Matilda to look for love. She found it in Sam, just as she was turning seventeen. The two quickly fell in love, finding solace in their unique psychological challenges. With eating disorders that leaned toward anorexia, both women craved the feeling of being in control and super thin. But Sam's issues outweighed Matilda's by far. Sam was also addicted to marijuana and alcohol, which had led to her nearly failing out of college. From the start, Matilda acted as the rescuer for Sam, engaging her in activities she thought might move Sam's life in a better direction. With an almost maternal instinct, Matilda would wake early in the morning to prevent Sam from oversleeping and missing her classes. She also helped Sam complete her homework assignments.

Being a smart and diligent person, Matilda initially juggled her new responsibility of managing Sam while finishing high school, but eventually she broke under the pressure. She lost sight of herself, which began to manifest physically with random fainting spells that required medical attention. Finding that her blood pressure was abnormally low, she took medication to treat it. Matilda's mother had been a long-term alcoholic, and the decades of family issues gave Matilda some awareness of the danger in Sam's partying habits. But over time her problems increased, and Matilda started smoking weed and taking anxiety medication to calm her anxious feelings. While the teenage years are a common time to experiment with partying and drugs, Matilda's experience went beyond that. Before long, her anxiety medication intake had increased, and she soon discovered it was one of the only things that made her feel *normal*.

Mary stopped taking care of herself after her first experience with love addiction. She convinced herself that love addiction was no longer a problem when the infatuation with Jane started up again. Since she spent most of her time working or being with Jane, her world had narrowed so much that she'd left no room for friendships. As the problem escalated, and Mary was at her lowest point, she not only had no effective self-care system in place, she had no one to turn to for guidance.

I Love Myself—Really—I Have No Idea What You Are Talking About

Love addicts use love, relationships, sex, and romance to hide what they secretly feel: unlovable, unworthy, and empty without a partner. Buried under their addictive behaviors are loneliness, sadness, grief, anger, guilt, and shame. Once the core problem is addressed and the addiction to love is exposed, the love addict can explore its origins and eventually learn how to heal. But awareness is a prerequisite to the healing process.

Josie was completely unaware that she had self-esteem issues. An attractive, charismatic, and talented musician, she found much outside validation from her fans and from her success. When her relationship with Danielle crumbled, Josie found herself feeling unbearable pain. For months she was forced to sit with the feelings of unworthiness she had been distracting herself from her entire life.

Charley was very good at seducing women. Funny and kind, she was the kind of butch lesbian straight woman were attracted to, and Charley found this flattering. The ability to "turn" these women into "lesbians" or "bisexual women" filled her with pride. Over time, she became addicted to the power she felt when seducing "straight" women. When these women left her or returned to men, as they inevitably did, Charley would feel crushed again. But the dopamine and oxytocin rush she acquired from flirting was enough to keep her going. This built a false sense of self-esteen, something Charley was completely unaware of. As is the case with any drug, the body develops a tolerance to the chemicals, so once flirting wasn't giving Charley the same high, her failing marriage took a bad turn.

Mary was attractive and successful in many areas of her life, including her career. She formed most of her self-esteem from being smart and from being good at her job. Despite years of therapy and a lot of personal work devoted to coming out, she had still managed to mask her low self-esteem and repress the feeling of being unlovable, especially from herself.

Never Alone

Unable to tolerate being alone, many love addicts will jump from relationship to relationship, taking no responsibility for why the last one didn't work and pursuing the high of a new romance at all costs. Some will have long periods between relationships, which they use to convince themselves that they have no problem being alone. But in reality, many are recovering from the trauma of their last disastrous experience.

Josie had been married to Anna for over six years when Anna started drinking again. They had met in recovery while dealing with serious substance abuse issues and were attracted to each other in part because of their shared respect for sobriety. Josie was not aware of how much Anna's falling out of recovery and returning to alcohol hurt her. In denial about the situation, she started fantasizing about Danielle, the hot, charismatic lead singer of their successful all-girl band. Josie was the band's guitarist. At first, the flirting between the two seemed harmless, until one night in Josie's car it went further and they couldn't keep their hands off each other. The sex was hot, and every window filled up with steam. Because Josie was married, they promised to consider it a one-time thing. When it happened again the following week, Josie's affair with Danielle officially began while Anna's affair with wine was already in full swing.

The relationship between Josie and Danielle became more and more dramatic as time went on and each woman's jealousy and insecurities grew. The band suffered as Josie and Danielle's long, heated discussions held them back from rehearsing. Eventually, the other band members tired of the situation and complained. At the same time, Danielle's jealousy about Josie's marriage went into overdrive, and when Josie couldn't take it anymore she told Anna about the relationship. They split up and Anna moved out. It was around this time that Josie came to me for therapy.

LOVE AVOIDANTS

What you are about to read is not going to make love avoidants sound good. But love avoidants, like addicts, suffer from their behavior and not from who they are or appear to be. Like love addicts, love avoidants suffer from the trauma and pain of damaging life experiences that manifest in behavior that is divergent from the more typical patterns of love addiction. Simply put, a love avoidant's behavior is usually very hurtful, and this alone can earn them an unfavorable position in other's eyes. Any woman who has been romantically involved with a woman caught in the love avoidant style, and has been hurt repeatedly, will understand why people often find them unlikable. While your anger is understandable because of the pain you've experienced, it is my hope to shed some light on this type of love addiction so that you can avoid taking the love avoidant's behavior personally. So whether you have dated a full-blown love avoidant or you have found yourself behaving this way in some of your relationships, now is time to better understand this phenomenon and find help. It is important to understand that the hurtful or destructive behavior love avoidants use to distance themselves in relationships originates from their love addiction. Consumed by the addiction, the love avoidant uses distance and then criticism, and sometimes even emotional cruelty, to sabotage her relationship and free herself.

Love addict and love avoidant styles struggle with many of the same core issues—attachment difficulties, trauma from growing up in a heterocentric and heterosexist world, internalized lesbianphobia, addiction to the high of falling in love, and a desire to avoid pain at all costs. The maelstrom of trauma, unconscious self-loathing, and unhealthy coping strategies leads to this serious intimacy disorder.

Addicted to Seducing

The love avoidant's favorite stage of a relationship is the chase. Love avoidants experience so much pleasure in pursuing and seducing women because it makes them feel desirable and in control. They thrive on the power differential. Once the conquest is achieved and the honeymoon burns out, love avoidants typically lose interest or want out.

Because the chemical hit that fuels the conquest comes from the seduction and not the relationship itself, a love avoidant can tire of her prize once the honeymoon is over. For some, this can happen pretty quickly. For others, it might take months. They may promise undying love and commitment during the seduction and honeymoon phase. They truly believe they mean it each time they meet and seduce a new woman or return to a previous relationship. But the love avoidant is neither aware of her addiction and/or what motivates her behavior, so she relies on this seduction and rejection pattern despite the harm it causes her and her partners. The love avoidant convinces herself that *this* relationship might be the one, or that *this* time things will be different. Love avoidants often believe that they are able and willing to commit for life, and even surprise themselves when they can't keep their promise.

Tina was the quintessential seducer. Women found Tina sophisticated, incredibly charming, and irresistible. Tina not only liked challenges, she found them stimulating, especially women who were not initially interested in her. It excited Tina to have three to four women on her call list at one time. Tina was raised in a dysfunctional family and was a survivor of sexual abuse. Her childhood began with an alcoholic mother who abandoned her, and ended with a cold stepmother and dissociated father who were oblivious to the abuse. As an adult, Tina discovered that seducing women gave her a rush, and she found a way to avoid her childhood pain by using the hit she got from seduction to distract and reward her. The more women Tina seduced, the more her pleasure centers were stimulated, and the higher she would get. Pursuing multiple women at a time kept Tina busy, and the dopamine and oxytocin pumping inside her. Unaware she was a love avoidant, Tina fancied herself "special" in her ability to have multiple women hooked into her at one time. This juggling act kept her from ever having to truly face her childhood trauma.

Intensity Mistaken for Intimacy

As with love addicts, love avoidants also mistake intensity for intimacy. The mirage of closeness that the couple creates is deceptive and misleading. Nevertheless, many lesbians find it extremely addictive, but no one more so than the love avoidant. The initial intense feelings the lesbian feels for her new love interest gives a false sense of intimacy. The love avoidant believes she can trust a woman she has literally just met, thereby letting down her guard and jumping into something that usually creates feelings of being smothered later.

The Urge to Merge

As with love addicts, lesbian love avoidants also love to merge. They idealize their new love interests. In the beginning, love avoidants will also become preoccupied and spend an inordinate amount of time thinking about their love interests and longing to be with them. This "falling in love" process creates a physical high when the sexual attraction and romantic feelings begin and the brain releases large amounts of dopamine and oxytocin. Thoughts of being together forever are extremely common. The physical high drives an intense desire to merge with their new love interest. As the actual merging takes place, the continual release of dopamine and oxytocin that the women experience during physical and emotional connection increases. This *oxytocin fest* feels amazing for both women, and as these potent feelings intensify they are mistaken for true intimacy.

I Love You—Really

Like love addicts, love avoidants unconsciously fear abandonment and the ups and downs of an authentic intimate relationship. Unaware of these fears, love avoidants will leave the relationship first so they can avoid the pain of being left. They may leave suddenly with little or no explanation, or because they have found someone else. Typically, the breakup is preceded by emotional and sexual distancing. Being left requires an ability to tolerate feelings of shame and unworthiness, and love avoidants will do anything they can to avoid being put in this position. They will work hard to secure their power position, and by leaving first they avert the suffering that comes from feeling unlovable. They become experts at avoiding being abandoned.

The love avoidant's behavior will often look cold and calculating on the surface. Because she convinces herself that she's "just fallen out of love," she won't appear remorseful or conscious of her actions—or their consequences. Having a new woman to seduce allows her to suppress any feelings of loss or grief, allowing her to quickly move onto the next conquest. This type of lesbian love avoidant was cleverly portrayed in the character Shane in the television series *The L Word*. Shane was a prototypical love avoidant, a serial seducer who lived for the chase. At the height of her love avoidance, Shane abandoned her fiancé Carmen, leaving her at the altar with no explanation.

Jane was also a master seducer. Charismatic, attractive, and smart, she often had many women at a time interested in her. This included straight-identified women moving through their questioning phase. Jane truly believed she had fallen in love with most of the women she became involved with, but once she lost interest in a woman, she would question having ever been in love with them. Even as she engaged in avoidant behaviors to distance herself from her partners, she continued to believe she was committed to each one of them. Truthfully, intimacy terrified her.

Abandonment was a core psychological issue for Jane, and to protect herself from reliving that painful experience, she would initiate the abandonment in her relationships. While the distancing and critical behavior may start subtly, eventually it intensifies, and this shift causes the love addict in the relationship to feel desperate and crazy for suggesting that her partner is backing away. It is not uncommon for the lesbian backing away to deny that her feelings are changing, or to convince her partner that she's just "feeling insecure," when in reality a shift is occurring. This is how the love addiction trap is set, and a situation that is untenable for both women increases.

Whether she had ended it or her girlfriend had ended it, Jane felt more relief than pain by the time it was over. Usually by this point, Jane had already set her sights on another woman. You can imagine how Jane's budding interest in a new woman also made the breakup process easier—for her at least. Even when she didn't jump into a new relationship right away, the desire for a new woman had begun. To stave off any potential jealousy, Jane was skilled at convincing her new partner, and herself, that she never really loved the woman she had recently separated from.

Smothered Again?

Love avoidants are particularly sensitive to feeling smothered by their partners. This can result from their own childhood trauma, often from a needy, overprotective, and smothering mother. But it is not uncommon for love avoidants to feel smothered even when they have plenty of space and freedom. Love addiction creates this feeling in the love avoidant. It is a response to her own trauma and pain. As the honeymoon wanes and the love avoidant experiences resistance to everyday intimacy, she may become disgusted by the not-so-charming parts of her partner and react by distancing herself from her. Feeling the love avoidant pull away triggers the love addict. Suddenly she wants more, needs more, and isn't sure why this shift is happening. Once she begins to ask for more (what she wants is to return to *the way things were*), her partner may see her as whiny or needy. This can create feelings of pressure that are too much to bear. To the lesbian on the receiving end, whose partner once appeared satisfied and stable, this causes panic.

Matilda eventually went into treatment for her anorexia nervosa. Luckily, we found a well-respected treatment center for adolescents, where she discovered she had a problem with marijuana and benzodiazepines (anxiety medication). After ninety days, Matilda came back dedicated to staying sober and abstinent from anorexia. Now she had a new problem. With two other addictions taken away from her, her love addiction took over. Upon her return home from treatment, her relationship with Sam picked right back up. Despite Sam's problem with using, they stayed together and became profoundly attached to each other. Around this time Matilda's love avoidance also presented itself.

THE LESBIAN LOVE ADDICTION SPIRAL BEGINS

A woman who is unaware of love addiction, as well as the love addict's intense sensitivity to abandonment, may begin to feel stuck with a woman who will never be satisfied. The thing is, she is right. Love addicts addicted to how good the merging feels to them will have an insatiable need for love, validation, and sex. This only gets worse when they begin to feel their partner slip away and become emotionally distant. Feeling smothered and scared by the intense merging, the love avoidant withdraws from the connection, which can take place gradually or quickly. The decrease in the feel-good chemicals is more tolerable to her because she *wants to stop merging*. She starts finding fault in her partner, maintaining distance, emotionally and sexually, and she can become overly critical. She will start belittling her partner to push her away and to avoid feeling even more smothered. Her core childhood attachment issues of abandonment are avoided because she still controls the power dynamic. The crazy train has not only left the station, it's traveling at high speed!

Once Josie was free to date Danielle openly, Danielle started acting differently. She was less available and wouldn't always answer her phone when Josie called. Josie started to panic. She was addicted with Danielle and couldn't wait to be with her. Danielle's change in attitude was extremely confusing. The first couple of times she confronted Danielle with the problem, it was resolved with wild sex and fun, impromptu weekends away. But after several drama-filled love addiction episodes, Danielle did not want to be with Josie anymore. She started feeling smothered and didn't like how intense Josie was behaving. From Danielle's perspective, they were only "fooling around," and besides, Josie had just left a marriage. Danielle didn't want to get pulled into that mess. So, instead of breaking up, she started sleeping with the band's drummer behind Josie's back.

I Love Being in a Long-Term Relationship

Love avoidants want love just like everybody else. What separates them is the trauma they experienced and haven't resolved. Love avoidants are addicted to the high of seduction, and the power that comes with that. But being repulsed by the idea (or reality) of being smothered, they back away. They are deathly afraid of dealing realistically with the ups and downs of authentic intimacy, and because they don't have the tools to deal with a relationship once the initial excitement wears off, they unconsciously start behaving differently in order to create distance. This keeps them in control and frees them from having to accept a woman who is less than perfect. Real intimacy comes from an understanding that everyone has lovable and unlovable qualities. Real intimacy occurs between two women who can truly accept each other's imperfections and accept each other's faults.

While Charley thought she could hide her daily porn habit from her wife, eventually her secret was discovered. It was a betrayal her wife could not overcome, despite the fact that she had not wanted to have sex with Charley in years. What mattered most to her was the feeling of being cheated on. Their fragile relationship was crumbling. Charley returned to her intriguing at work to help counteract the fear and hurt she felt from problems in her relationship. She still loved her wife, the thought of losing her was terrifying, but she could not control her urges. Then she met Sandra. Sandra was a very sexy and attractive woman who frequented the iconic restaurant where Charley worked. She and Sandra started flirting heavily, and it soon moved to a physical relationship. While Charley was moving from the ten-year home she had shared with her wife into a small studio apartment, the high she experienced with Sandra made the trauma of losing her marriage and home go away. She was enthralled and soon became obsessed. All she could think about was Sandra. She began living for their secret trysts. However, Sandra identified as straight and didn't want anyone to know she and Charley were in a relationship. Charley didn't mind at first because she loved seducing straight women. She found the secrecy exhilarating, but over time it started to erode her sense of self as she realized she longed for more than just a covert relationship with an unavailable woman.

THE LESBIAN LOVE ADDICT MERGER

Figure 4.1 is a diagram to help illustrate how the lesbian love addiction merger occurs. Each category applies to the different aspects of the love addict and the love avoidant explained earlier.

As the merging period began to shift for Mary and Jane, Jane found herself more and more frustrated with Mary. She found her once cute idiosyncrasies unbearable. Over time, everything about Mary started to annoy her, from the way she ate to the way she dressed to the way she liked to have sex. Feeling suffocated by Mary's needs, Jane found herself pulling further and further away. Unequipped to deal with these new unpleasant feelings, Jane suddenly became very critical of Mary and was not feeling physically drawn to her like she used to. Losing interest in sex confused Jane and caused her to question her sexuality. What was wrong with her? Was she straight—or just unsure of herself? How could she feel so indifferent toward someone she once wanted to marry? Detaching was the only way she knew how to calm the anxiety this confusion created in her. When detaching herself seemed to work, and she found herself intrigued by a woman she had only recently become friends with, Jane discovered a way out.

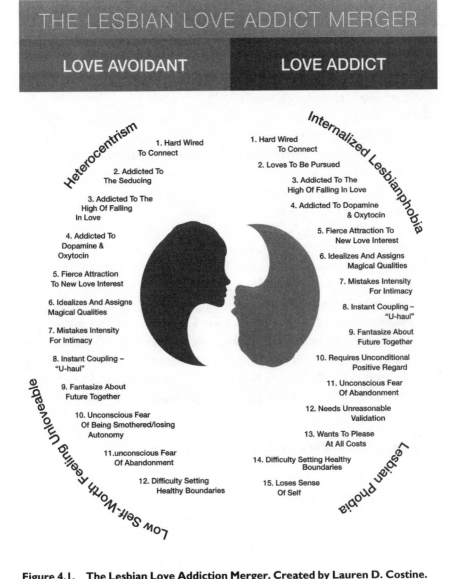

Figure 4.1. The Lesbian Love Addiction Merger. Created by Lauren D. Costine. Designed by Jen Baers/Studio 10 Designs.

The Lesbian Love Addiction Descent

Whether you see yourself as a love addict, a love avoidant, notice a little of each of these characteristics in your behavior, or have been both at one time or another, the most important discovery you can make is to recognize the trap of lesbian love addiction. You know the urge to merge is powerful. The merging is exhilarating and full of new and exciting experiences, but once the longing has been satisfied and replaced with reality, or when the merge no longer works, difficult feelings arise. Once the break in the connection occurs, fear, anxiety, distancing, anger, and resentment begin to replace the excitement and rush that began the relationship.

The unhealthy merger creates a spiral that is powerful enough to suck both women to an even deeper, more destructive place. Minor disconnects become serious, drama escalates, fights ensue, sex dwindles, and authentic communication feels impossible. Sometimes this happens gradually, but once each woman is in her own unique form of pain that the other can't understand, the spiral progresses quickly and becomes overwhelming.

Once a relationship hits this point, repairing the problems can be difficult, even in couple's therapy. Unfortunately, as with many addictions, therapy is not a guaranteed "cure." Of course, having a professional to discuss the issues with is an important element of the healing process, but healing from lesbian love addiction requires a therapist who thoroughly understands this affliction and possesses a deep knowledge of its root causes. There is still a great need for books, treatment centers, and other love addiction support systems to address lesbian love addiction from a lesbian-affirmative perspective.

Characteristics of the Lesbian Love Addiction Spiral

- Love avoidant tires of merging and the love addict's need for unconditional positive regard.
- Love avoidant initiates first subtle, or ever so slight, emotional break in merging.
- Love addict is acutely aware of the slightest loss of merging qualities and starts to demand it back (verbally or energetically). Her fear of abandonment escalates. She is frightened by the power that she believes the love avoidant has over her.
- Love avoidant is averse to any signs of smothering. Acute awareness of her partner's "neediness" causes her to pull further away.
- Love addict is now looking for any small sign of emotional distancing. She panics (internally or as a physical response).

- The partner's panicked state causes the love avoidant to pull further away. Affection and sex become more and more sporadic.

THE LESBIAN LOVE ADDICTION SPIRAL

It is common for couples to get back together to avoid the feelings of withdrawal that this addiction creates. After getting back together, the merger and spiral reappears as many times as it takes for the relationship to end permanently. However, it doesn't stop here. The merger and spiral will reappear in the next relationship if the love addiction is not addressed.

Once Tina found herself back in a relationship with Mary, which was initially exhilarating and calming, she began to feel sick and full of dread, and she realized that she couldn't be in a relationship at this time. Mary just needed her too much. At first she would find herself physically ill, exhausted by the seduction phase as her feel-good chemicals stopped producing—overused and burned out—and she would go into major withdrawals without knowing it. Like a heroin addict who cannot get any more heroin or doesn't want to do it anymore, withdrawals are quick and dirty. To her, she was just sick because she had once again overcommitted by agreeing to help Mary with whatever crisis she was dealing with at the time. Ever the consummate rescuer, Tina would put aside all her needs and run to help whenever Mary needed her. Helping Mary made her feel useful and productive, but once she had to turn her attention back to her own life she would crash—physically and emotionally. Around this time she would realize she needed space and would inevitably call Mary and start to backpedal on all her previous promises of devotion and happily ever after. She knew she couldn't deliver and she was too tired to worry about it. She just wanted out.

Understandably, Matilda started to fear Sam's using, which had gotten out of control. She also struggled with the fact that Sam would not come out. Sam's bisexuality was not the problem for Matilda. In fact, she supported Sam's identity, but she was bothered that they kept their relationship a secret from Sam's lesbianphobic and biphobic family. As Matilda put pressure on Sam to decrease her drug use and come out to her family, she began to find flirtatious texts from men Sam met at college parties. When she would confront Sam, Sam said they were

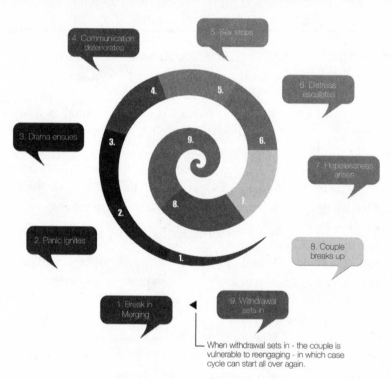

Figure 4.2.   The Lesbian Love Addiction Spiral. Created by Lauren D. Costine.

nothing. The love addiction spiral had begun, and both women were stuck in it. Matilda started dreading having sex with Sam. Matilda's continued rejections were devastating to Sam. Each week Matilda would find herself recoiling from Sam's overtures. This made her feel horrible as she loved Sam but could not find her way back to feeling attracted to her. Matilda, understanding the benefits of therapy and recovery, was immediately receptive to our work around her love addiction. She was also open to looking at her love avoidant behaviors with Sam. As part of looking at her childhood trauma and attachment issues, we started intensive work around her mother. Her mother was the ambivalent type—sometimes loving and available, and at other times completely absent either because she was drunk or because she was distracted by her own dysfunctional marriage to Matilda's father. While the spiral with Sam became irreparable, Matilda stayed dedicated to her lesbian-affirmative love addiction work and started to process what she needed to do to take care of herself.

HOW LOVE ADDICTS AND LOVE AVOIDANTS FIND EACH OTHER

By now you hopefully understand why love addicts and love avoidants attract each other and are in relationships together. Conversely, these roles can switch during the course of a relationship. Sex addiction pioneer Patrick Carnes calls this union and its rotating nature the *trauma bond*. In his book, *The Betrayal Bond: Breaking Free of Exploitive Relationships*, he offers a grim description of the psychological interaction that takes place in a trauma bond. "A form of abandonment. Often the abandonment is difficult to see because the betrayer can be still close, even intimate, or may be intruding in your life. Yet your interests, your well-being is continually sacrificed. . . . Abandonment is at the core of addictions. Abandonment causes deep shame. Abandonment by betrayal is worse than mindless neglect. Betrayal is purposeful and self-serving."[10] As awful as this sounds, it makes sense in the context of love addiction and the trajectory it typically takes. The minute the two women first see each other, they might experience love at first sight. This sensation, the rush, feels familiar, and because both woman are wounded and addicted to merging, they forge an unconscious contract. Neither woman is aware of her addiction to the high of falling in love, her insatiable need to attach, or the patterns she will automatically act out. Neither woman is conscious of the dynamic they create together, or that they can't resist it. Pia Mellody describes the union of the love addict and the love avoidant in *Facing Love Addiction*:

With all this conflict, it may seem strange that these people could ever have been attracted to each other. But it is important to note that each person is first attracted to the other specifically because of the "familiar" traits the other exhibits. These traits, although painful, are familiar from child abuse experiences. [11]

We saw this both with Mary and Tina and with Mary and Jane. Mary experienced "love at first sight" with each woman, or so she thought. She did experience an immediate connection and could not forget them once the first contact was made. The good news about this dynamic is that when the pain becomes great enough, it can force one to wake up, and it offers each woman the opportunity to heal. Unfortunately, for many women, the pain is the only thing that propels us to seek help and finally end the cycle.

What is important to remember is that each woman is unconsciously trying to recover those early childhood needs, those that were withheld by the mother and were being met by her new love. Because these unfulfilled emotional needs are unconscious, the women are unaware of the pressure this puts on their partner and on the relationship. Over time, neither woman can fulfill the fantasy of being the savior, or live up to the expectation that her partner must become her everything.

Neither woman can shoulder the blame for these fantasies. The culture of media and pop music we exist in reinforces the notion that this is the way love is supposed to be. Love will make us happy, love will heal our childhood, love is the answer to everything. The messages we receive about coupling are unrealistic, idealized, and unattainable. Nevertheless, many lesbian love addicts unconsciously buy into the idea that love will erase their accumulated pain, and they rely heavily on their relationships to make it a reality over and over and over again. When each relationship ends in drama, the pain intensifies, and the love addiction grows. As the addiction grows, the inevitable sense of hopelessness and distress sets in. Like the infant we witnessed in the strange situation experiment, the love addict feels abandoned, unloved, and unlovable, and she responds with fear and anxious behavior. What she is actually experiencing is the feeling of withdrawal. We'll explore this phenomenon in greater detail in the next chapter.

INTIMACY AND SEXUAL ANOREXIA

In my practice I work with lesbians who suffer from a distinct kind of love avoidance, which in the field we call *sexual anorexia*. Derived from the well-known eating disorder anorexia, this term explains what can happen when one's avoidance of intimacy and sex becomes so acute a type of starvation occurs. Two heterosexually based books have been written on this topic, Patrick Carnes's *Sexual Anorexia: Overcoming Sexual Self-Hatred* and Douglas Weiss's *Intimacy Anorexia: Healing the Hidden Addiction in Your Marriage*. Their research began when these psychologists noticed that straight men who had recovered from sex addiction displayed an unanticipated new problem: complete sexual avoidance of their wives. They realized through their work with these men that they all displayed a phobia toward authentic intimacy. Carnes's book discusses the problems that can occur when someone avoids relationships altogether, while both books highlight what happens when these characteristics show up in long-term relationships, causing much pain for both partners stuck in the anorexic vortex. This is similar to what happens in the lesbian love addiction spiral. The love avoidant's fear of being smothered by her anxious partner causes her to recoil physically and emotionally. As this occurs, the sexual anorexia in the relationship is ignited and their intimacy disorders are heightened.

Anorexia, like addiction, controls one's hunger while creating a high for the anorexic. This type of addict gets a "hit" from the restrictive behaviors and the ability to control her urges. By denying their own urges, sexual anorexics have power over their partners, and this feeling replaces the need for affection, touch, and sex. In the same way that controlling one's food feels empowering, sex, which is also a source of enjoyment and pleasure, when controlled and avoided feels better to the sexual anorexic.[12] This happens at least for a while because with the relief of avoiding intimacy comes pain, frustration, and loneliness. This is the time when a lesbian who suffers from these issues might seek help.

Matilda began to resist Sam's touch and her desire for sex. Restricting contact with Sam made her feel more in control of a relationship that had spun out of control. Matilda was also fueled by a growing resentment that Sam was being unfaithful, but there were deeper issues to blame for this increasing feeling of distrust. Matilda had been sexually molested at the age of seven and spent most of her childhood blaming herself for the incident. Her mother could be loving and enormously affirming of her daughter's lesbianism at one moment but then emotionally unreliable the next. Subsequently, Matilda guarded her emotions and avoided any kind of vulnerability to protect herself. Once the bloom of their first love had faded and the love addiction spiral was in full force, Matilda pulled away from Sam but still wanted to be with her all the time. As she became more and more distant emotionally and sexually, their problems felt unresolvable.

Intimacy Anorexics Who Are Single

Some lesbian anorexics attempt dating, but the attempts are often unsuccessful and frustrating. They resist new opportunities by finding the woman unattractive or they gravitate toward women who aren't attracted to them. They have a hard time connecting and find relationships, in general, challenging. Their attachment issues make connections seem unappealing, and their brain chemistry doesn't create pleasure when they do connect with another woman, thus they avoid it.

Many lesbians troubled by sexual anorexia spend much of their lives alone. This is different from asexuality. People who identify as asexual don't long to be in a relationship; they are happy and satisfied with their single life.[13] Lesbians who suffer from anorexia are not happy or satisfied with being alone. They would love to be in a relationship, but their intense fear of intimacy blocks them from finding one. This behavior is usually unconscious and can go on for years untreated, until the pain becomes so great they are forced to seek help. The research by sexual anorexic specialists show there is hope for recovery. When attention is given to the avoidance and fears of intimacy and internal space, recovery is attainable. SLAA has specific meetings that help love addicts who suffer from this issue. There are also psychotherapists and addiction specialists certified in treating sex addiction who are specially trained to work with this issue. If you relate to any part in this section, professionals can help.

Maria, an athletic Latina lesbian, had not been in a relationship for over ten years. She dated on multiple occasions but had a hard time finding anyone she was attracted to for more than one or two dates. Her difficulty in finding a mate caused her much distress. She really desired a soul mate, and did not want to spend the rest of her life alone, but she had no idea how to change her predicament. After years of working on her issues with her mother, her childhood trauma, and her family's unrelenting lesbianphobia, I helped her find a sexual anorexic women's support group. While mixed in its sexual orientation, she found sharing her feelings with the other eight women in the group each week helpful. As trust developed, the women pointed out unhealthy guarded behavior that many of them fell back into. They held each other accountable for their actions. Today Maria is dating again, attending local lesbian meet-up events, and her dating profile is back online.

The Infamous Lesbian Bed Death

Charley had been with her wife for over ten years when her love addiction started to cause significant problems. For six of their ten years together, Charley, and her wife had stopped having sex altogether.

In the 1983 book *American Couples*, sociologist Pepper Schwartz and Phillip Blumstein fatefully coined the term "lesbian bed death" to describe what happens in some lesbian relationships.[14] In a study conducted by Schwartz and Blumstein, the researchers found that lesbians in long-term committed relationships had less sex than any of their counterparts (heterosexual women and men and gay men). *American Couples* also erroneously claimed that lesbians were less adventurous and less technically skilled in the bedroom. Since then, thankfully, the study's methodology has been questioned and numerous books have argued these findings. However, the damage was done, and the term haunts the lesbian community to this day. The deleterious consequences of that myth have unfortunately been allowed to remain in the consciousness of many lesbians who continue to believe it is inevitable in a committed relationship. It has also made its way into the lesbian lexicon that both the straight and LGBTQ community employ. Truthfully, all relationships, heterosexual and LGBTQ, are vulnerable to sexual anorexia when an intimacy disorder and the love addiction spiral are at work.

As in the lesbian love addiction spiral, sexual and intimacy anorexia usually occur in relationships where love addiction is present. Whatever the symptoms, this is an intimacy disorder. While Schwartz's study was flawed in multiple ways, the most damage was created by the researchers' lack of understanding about lesbian trauma and love addiction. With the awareness that perhaps a number of the study's participants may have been love addicts, my hope is that this term will be reevaluated as a problem and taken out of the lesbian community's lexicon and instead be seen as the complex intimacy disorder that it is.

DOMESTIC VIOLENCE IN LESBIAN RELATIONSHIPS

Love addictions can involve a lot of deception, manipulation, controlling behavior, and jealousy. These behaviors are not the bedrock of mental health. Since a relationship between the love addict and love avoidant is built on the urge to merge, the addiction to falling in love, the intensity, and the lure of feel-good chemicals their bodies produce, authentic intimacy is not developed. The absence of authentic intimacy leads to enormous insecurity, which can fuel jealousy and escalate into rages and emotionally manipulative behavior brought on by a deeper need to control the partner. Imagine how crazy things can get when a fragile relationship reaches this point. Several studies have shown that 24–90 percent of white, educated, middle-class lesbians have reported experiencing psychological abuse at least once in their relationship.[15] Sadly, all of this behavior is really just a very dysfunctional strategy used to get unmet needs met. Initially the desire to merge and the subtle intonations of jealousy can look like blossoming love, when in fact they are symptoms of love addiction. Over time, the jealousy or possessiveness that was once flattering or cute stops being so and these behaviors damage the trust and integrity of the relationship. Love-addicted relationships can also grow more extreme, and in some cases even result in violent acts and physical harm. There is a dangerous myth out there that promotes the idea that lesbians can't have violent relationships, but that is not the case. In 2000, studies showed that about 17–45 percent of lesbians reported being victims of at least one violent attack by a partner.[16] Thankfully, organizations like the Los Angeles LGBT Center are dedicated to treating lesbian couples who find themselves experiencing domestic violence.

WHAT HAPPENS NEXT

Love addiction is painful for everyone involved. Because it manifests differently in each person and in each relationship, women should recognize and understand its origins. Love avoidants and love addicts suffer from the same issues, though each hurts the other differently. Thinking that love avoidants escape pain by leaving early is wrong. The emotional pain that love avoidants experience may be less obvious, but they too suffer. Running from one relationship to another may seem like the quick and easy way to avoid feelings of abandonment, but love avoidants can be sober from this addiction and experience terrible withdrawals during the healing process. Once they learn how to stop using seduction, power, and relationships to medicate their trauma and attachment issues, years of avoiding the underlying causes of this addictive behavior surface, and it is hard, but worth it, to work through this, as you'll see in the next chapter.

Now that you understand the underlying reasons behind lesbian love addiction and how it manifests in our behaviors, now is the time to learn how to heal. The rest of this book will focus on how to heal from love addiction. Next, we will look at love addiction withdrawal, from the initial symptoms of it to hitting bottom and the final stages of the withdrawal. Healing is not possible without this component. In chapter 6, we will explore how to create a healthy relationship with yourself before starting a new relationship with another. Then we will discuss healthy dating tips and how to create a healthy relationship once you have found someone to be in a relationship with.

5

WITHDRAWAL

What It is and How It Benefits Us

Parting is all we know of heaven and all we need to know of hell.
—Emily Dickinson [1]

Mary came into my office barely able to contain her tears. She was referred to me because she heard I worked with lesbians who were dealing with painful breakups. She initially told me she was feeling worse since her breakup and she didn't understand what was happening to her. She felt anxious all the time, and nothing seemed to calm her. She felt like she was "going to die," and this really scared her. She didn't want to take her own life, but she also didn't want to live this way, feeling stuck and hopeless. She worried that she was "going crazy" and wondered if going to a hospital would help stop the pain she was experiencing. I listened as she described her relationship with Jane in detail, the initial crazy falling in love period, the insane attraction and great sex, the constant texting, then the emotional distancing, the critical comments, and the physical and sexual rejections. It was almost impossible for her to say it, but she knew her heart had been broken.

After several sessions, I quietly stated, "The pain you are experiencing over this breakup is so normal but the behavior you are describing with Jane sounds very addictive." Mary paused, became quiet, and I waited to see if this would make sense to her or cause her to pull away. Then she exclaimed, "Oh my god, you are right. It was *so* addictive!" She bolted up from the couch and launched into more detail about her experiences in SLAA and with Tina and Sophie. "I can't believe this," she said, "how did I not see it? I mean I'm a love addict, a serious, full-blown love addict!" "Denial can be pretty powerful," I replied.

MARY'S JOURNEY THROUGH WITHDRAWAL

Mary's pain didn't go away after that eye-opening session, but it did start her on the road to recovery. While her pain lasted for many more months, she at least understood what was happening—finally. She no longer felt like admitting herself into a hospital because she thought she was insane or dying. AA helped her get sober in the past, so she decided to return to SLAA and see what might happen. She immediately found a sponsor, attended as many meetings as she could, and established what SLAA calls "bottom lines." Soon she was working the steps. Each day was painful, but she continued to hope. It took every ounce of energy she had to get through each day, but she powered on. I explained to her the physical components of withdrawal and assured her that it would be over one day. From an intellectual perspective she believed me, but her heart took almost a year to catch up. Fortunately, Mary was motivated to heal and be done with denial. She understood she was a love addict and, for her, there was no going back.

Stopping love addiction behavior has its own withdrawal effects, just like stopping alcohol or heroin. Thanks to the research and knowledge we have today, we know that Mary was experiencing withdrawal much like what happens when a person stops drinking or using. The difference with love addiction, however, is that for many the withdrawal can last much longer.

WHAT IS WITHDRAWAL FROM LOVE?

Humans have been writing about it for thousands of years. The loss of love is a universal human experience. Countless poems, paintings, films, TV shows, and songs illustrate the pain associated with a broken heart. Sappho spoke about it in one of her poems—writing how she felt like a part of her was dying as she watched a woman she was in love with marry a man.[2] While it is not a medical term, the word *broken* describes what one is *actually* feeling inside when romantic love is gone. Many people have thought they were dying when a relationship ended. One colloquialism passed down for centuries is "dying from a broken heart." Researchers and doctors have called this experience of devastating loss the "broken heart syndrome" because it does have physiological symptoms that, for many, can feel like a heart attack.[3] Dr. Wittstein from Johns Hopkins University has been studying the phenomenon for decades. He found that while breakups have the hallmark symptoms of grief, which will be explored shortly, it is now known to affect the SNS, activating the "flight or fight" system. In this condition, the body releases a number of chemicals, including adrenaline, that can cause the heart to work harder than usual. Interestingly, the studies on this syndrome show that 90 percent of the cases were women (the study does not indicate the women's sexual orientation).[4]

Love addiction withdrawal is not treated as a singular condition that is taught in the field of psychology, or recognized in the *DSM-5*, but recent studies have shown the deleterious effects on the brain when someone we love rejects us. One such study by Dr. Helen Fisher and her colleagues presented heartbroken heterosexual participants pictures of their loved ones. Each participant was given social psychologists Hatfield and Sprecher's 1986 Passionate Love Scale (PLS). This scale is designed to measure the cognitive, emotional, and behavioral features relating to the feelings for a current or former romantic partner.[5] Afterwards, MRI scans of their brains were taken, blood was drawn, and participants' emotional reactions were recorded. While looking at the photo of a former partner, each participant showed physiological signs of stress and subsequently reported feeling distress, fear, sadness, hopelessness, anger, desire for revenge, or despair. These studies continue and have been very helpful for the social and clinical psychologists and medical researchers trying to understand what happens to us physically when we experience romantic loss or rejection. These studies help validate and provide empirical evidence for ideas that psychologists, healers, artists, and poets have been purporting for thousands of years.

Luckily we exist at a time in history when studies of the brain have become instrumental in helping us understand the mental, physical, and emotional effects of breakups. With a more biological perspective, we can measure the effect this kind of loss has on our hearts and minds.

We also know much more about withdrawal from addiction. Together these studies provide a great deal of knowledge about the physiology of withdrawal, both from a relationship and from an addiction perspective. Knowledge is power, and this insight can offer those suffering from love addiction withdrawal a clearer idea of what is happening in their bodies. The science of withdrawal has been misunderstood and misjudged for many years, and now we are closer to knowing the facts.

As described in earlier chapters, we now know much more about the neurochemical components of falling in love and what happens when we become deeply attached to our romantic partners. We also know how women are physiologically and hormonally wired to connect. Knowing that love omits the most intoxicating of chemicals, dopamine and oxytocin, while activating multiple areas of the brain that bring pleasure and a sense of security, makes it easier to understand how a sudden, and in the case of love addiction brutal, removal of these elements can have catastrophic consequences.

Although we don't yet have all the data on what happens when a person experiences withdrawal from love addiction, we do have material that explains its trajectory. We also have books such as *Facing Love Addiction*, *Breaking Your Addiction to a Person*, and SLAA's core text, which have helped inform this book. These texts describe the phenomenon of withdrawal from love addiction well. Calling withdrawal "the gateway to freedom," the founder of SLAA, who remains anonymous, says it best in the SLAA basic text:

> The pain of withdrawal is unique, special, even precious (although you probably don't now think so). In a sense, the experience is you, a part of you which has been trying to surface for a long time. You have been avoiding or postponing this pain for a long time now, yet you have never been able to lastingly outrun it. You need to go through withdrawal in order to become a whole person. You need to meet yourself. Behind the terror of what you fear, withdrawal contains the seeds for your own personal wholeness. It must be experienced for you to realize, or make real, that potential for you and your life which has been stored there for so long.[6]

We know that withdrawing from love addiction usually entails a break-up, the catalyst that alerts the person to the problem; we also know that the breakup is not nearly as painful as the process of getting "sober" from love addiction. When one stops the addictive behavior and goes into withdrawal, physiological and psychological losses occur. People in alcohol and heroin detox often experience an increase in agitation, anger, anxiety, crying, insomnia, and depression.[7] These are the same symptoms that love addicts experience in the early stages of withdrawal.

Keeping in mind the diagnostic criterion that describes addiction from the last chapter, let's look at some examples of behavior that many (though not all) lesbian love addicts engage in when experiencing or trying to avoid withdrawal. These can include:

- Seducing and chasing women outside your committed relationship
- Staying in an unhappy relationship and avoiding working on the issues
- Having sex outside of your committed relationship
- Chasing women who are unavailable
- Jumping right into another relationship following a breakup
- Fantasizing and idealizing women without knowing them
- Obsessing over one person
- Stalking or stopping by your ex's unannounced
- Cyberstalking or following a person's social media activity
- Making constant and unwanted texts, e-mails, and phone calls
- Returning to the same unhealthy relationship over and over again
- Flirting and intriguing with multiple women
- Compulsive pornography use
- Compulsive masturbation
- Game playing, manipulation, and control tactics
- Taking care of others instead of yourself

Not all of these are maladaptive in and of themselves—flirting, falling in love, and healthy dependency in relationships are important. These behaviors make life enjoyable. Couples need to develop a healthy dependency on each other to strengthen their connection. The key word here is *healthy*. Love and sex are important parts of life, which are meant to be enjoyed. Sexual repression is not healthy for any of us, and a sex-positive attitude is paramount to a balanced life. But often in isolation or when in a love-addicted relationship, these behaviors cause problems, especially when they become compulsive and repeated attempts to stop have failed. At this point these behaviors belong in the love addiction category.

This chapter will highlight love addiction withdrawal, while incorporating all we've learned so far about the unique physiology that women share and the psychology that inhabits the lesbian mind. We will also follow Mary, Charley, Matilda, Josie and a few others on their journey toward recovery.

HOW TO GET SOBER FROM LOVE ADDICTION

In many ways, withdrawal is the most important concept in this book. This is because withdrawing from lesbian love addiction is the key to recovering from this debilitating addiction—and changing your life. The good news about love addiction is withdrawal does not mean abstinence from all the behaviors associated with love forever. Actually, love addicts often find love once they have recovered. Initially abstinence is helpful and highly recommended for recovery. But engaging in love and sex in healthy and fulfilling ways is an important goal for your future.

Bottom Lines

In SLAA (sometimes pronounced SLAW), the first step in getting well from love addiction is done by setting your bottom lines.[8] These are like personal rules or boundaries we create to discourage our own unhealthy behaviors.

Because they vary from woman to woman, every set of bottom lines is different and personal to each love addict's problematic behaviors. For example, a lesbian love addict might decide not to have any contact with her ex-girlfriend for any reason or to not engage with women who are unavailable on her bottom-line list.

In SLAA, the person that initiated your need to get into the program is called a *qualifier*.[9] This term is also used in Al-Anon and refers to the person who initially triggered your need to seek help and guidance from a twelve-step program. The love addict's qualifier would be the person or the ex she is texting and calling weeks or months after they've broken up. Engaging in these behaviors makes her feel worse, but she feels unequipped to stop them. The ex is no longer interested, and yet the love addict keeps putting herself in the position of being repeatedly rejected. Since rejection and abandonment are major triggers, this behavior becomes almost masochistic.

Since many love addicts find it extremely difficult to stop these behaviors without support, the bottom-line protocol provides a guide for making it happen. Just as an addict or alcoholic is in need of removing an addictive substance, a love addict learns to refrain from engaging with that person, the qualifier, no matter what. Stopping these destructive behaviors elicits painful withdrawal symptoms and can be extremely challenging, but sticking to the bottom lines is an imperative part of recovering and making room for a healthy sense of self and future healthy relationships. Common bottom-line behaviors are discussed below.

No Contact

One of the most effective ways to heal from a love-addicted relationship is to employ a *no contact* rule.[10] For some addicts, the pain of the breakup becomes so unbearable that breaking all contact is easy. This occurs when you realize that contacting your ex (or qualifier) causes you more pain than relief. For some, creating a no contact agreement with the help of a twelve-step program, therapist, or support group comes rather naturally. For others, stronger tools are needed to create this boundary.

When Mary finally realized she was a love addict, her first bottom line was to cut off all contact with Jane. They had been periodically corresponding since Jane moved out. Mary realized that their occasional phone calls, voicemail messages, and e-mails to discuss each other's sadness over the breakup were keeping her from completely withdrawing from Jane and moving on. Jane's voice sounded different—the affectionate tone she had come to rely on since they became romantically involved was gone. Jane was talking to her like she was just a friend, not her previous "soul mate." She understood why Jane needed to do this, but it still triggered all her abandonment attachment issues. She e-mailed Jane and told her she had finally realized she was a love addict and could no longer have any sort of contact with her. The e-mail gave Mary immense relief as she realized the e-mails and phone calls with Jane were not helping her recover.

Charley's first bottom line was to cut off all contact with her qualifier, Sandra, the unavailable woman she had been having an on again, off again affair with for months. It was hard for Charley at first. She found herself texting her qualifier whenever she was feeling lonely, bored, or happy. However, with the help of her sponsor, she developed a system where she would call her sponsor or friends in SLAA whenever she had the urge to contact her qualifier. Initially, this intensified Charley's withdrawal symptoms, which included insomnia, agitation, anxiety, and bouts of depression, but as she attended meetings and reached out to her safe friends, the urges to call her qualifier eventually disappeared. This was an enlightening moment for Charley. When she realized she no longer wanted to call her qualifier, Charley experienced a sense of freedom she had never felt before.

No Seducing or Chasing

Another example of a love avoidant's bottom line might be *no seducing or chasing any women or no seducing or intriguing with women outside the committed relationship for any reason.* Drawing this line is typically very difficult at first, but by changing this behavior the love avoidant is preventing herself from using other women to get *high* and to make herself feel better. It is an imperative first step toward living with integrity. Over time, the love avoidant must learn to show interest in another woman only when she is truly interested and plans to follow through on her promises or stay faithful to a partner she has committed to. Lying and deceitful behavior unconsciously erodes one's sense of self, so putting this new behavior into practice helps the love avoidant build self-worth. Though the love avoidant achieves a sense of power and self-esteem from seducing women, the selfish nature of this act creates confusion and misunderstandings that lead to negative consequences.

Let's use Shane from *The L Word* as an example again.[11] Throughout the series, Shane would often seduce woman. After showering them with attention and sleeping with them, Shane would typically disappear. This is now known in popular twenty-first-century parlance as *ghosting*—when someone you have been dating disappears without explanation.[12] If she ran into them at The Planet or a local bar, these women would corner Shane and ask her why she hadn't called as promised. At this point she would usually lie and tell them she was still very interested and would be in touch as soon as she could. Of course she never did because Shane was a tried and true love avoidant. But no one can avoid pain altogether. The love avoidant may get high from the power they wield over others, but this behavior stems from a place of deep self-hatred, and over time, it fuels feelings of shame, unworthiness, lack of control, craziness, and selfishness. In *The L Word*, Shane would not talk about her behavior, but her lack of self-worth became evident as she hung her head in shame or disappeared from her friends to avoid being "seen" when she acted out her addictive behaviors.

Charley's other bottom line was to stop chasing and seducing women. She stopped this behavior at the same time she cut off all contact with her qualifier. She also realized she could never seduce and intrigue with other women once she was in her next relationship. She had used her addiction to comfort herself, and it had become harmful. Stopping all of these behaviors became a big part of her withdrawal experience.

After Matilda broke up with Sam, she was more relieved than anything else. But as she created her own bottom lines, she started feeling the pangs of withdrawal. To heal, Matilda knew she needed to completely cut off from Sam, and from seducing or chasing other women. She also knew there should be no rescuing of anyone with a substance abuse or love addiction. As her withdrawal symptoms emerged, the anxiety and fear resurfaced, but this time Matilda was determined that she would not turn to anxiety medication to calm her nerves. She was forced to utilize other forms of withdrawal relief such as attending twelve-step meetings, exercise, meditation, and allowing herself to be vulnerable with friends she trusted.

Valerie, who attended SLAA meetings for her recovery process, wished someone had told her that the first months would eventually pass. Those initial months made her feel like she was losing her mind. Coming off of love addiction was the hardest thing she had ever done. There were moments when she felt like she couldn't breathe. She also started going to therapy, journaling, taking mini day trips into nature, exercising, and calling other women in the program. Through all of this, she started to feel the pain shift around and open up inside of her. Thankfully, this was when her hope was restored.

No Dating

Another effective tool is to hold off on dating until you have healed, not just from your last relationship but from your love addiction as well.

Dating can work as a great distractor as it prevents you from the difficult inner work needed to truly heal. Not dating gives you the opportunity to look at your attachment patterns, possible trauma, family-of-origin issues, internalized lesbianphobia, and it can help you build authentic feelings of self-love and a healthier sense of self-worth. Imagine the kind of woman you will be once you have done this work and are ready to begin a new relationship.

No Fantasizing

For some lesbian love addicts, fantasizing about actresses, models, coworkers, and women walking down the street can be addictive. When fantasy is one of the behaviors that gets you high, stopping it can be a challenge. But once you understand that it is a device that really only offers temporary relief, its power decreases.

Starting with the beautiful blonde genie from *I Dream of Jeanie*, Mary had developed huge crushes on actresses, models, and female teachers since she was a child. As a young girl, she didn't recognize these feelings as crushes, she just knew that sometimes she was obsessed with women she saw on TV or in the movies or admired at school. Innately, she knew she could stare at these women without garnering negative attention. These crushes not only released dopamine into her system, they encouraged her fear of dealing with a real woman. By assigning them magical qualities, Mary created in her fantasy world a stable of perfect women. She dreamed of Jeanie over and over again!

One of the first bottom lines Mary created was to stop fantasizing about actresses. Creating these fantasy women had become second nature to her, but with hard work and some time to reflect on it, she found it easier to stop it from going too far. Luckily, she did not have to stop watching films or television altogether, just those that involved women she was intensely attracted to. Mary's withdrawal period lasted almost a year, mostly because there were many bottom-line behaviors she wanted to cross of her list. While Mary was recovering from her last addictive relationship with Jane, she also used this time to wean herself from the other unhealthy behaviors that activated her body's pleasure centers. Creating zero access to any of these addictive behaviors initially increased the withdrawal symptoms. While Mary felt normal and was noticeably calmer, she still experienced anxiety, insomnia, agitation, and depressive episodes over the first twelve months.

Josie had to stop imagining all her fans were perfect. In this fantasy world, Josie saw her fan base as women who were beautiful, adoring, easygoing, and needless. These made-up scenarios made her happy. Since she struggled with the less-than-charming parts of the women she loved, imaging that her fan's perfect personas were real was a welcome relief. Realizing through therapy that her desire for a perfect woman stemmed from her mother's emotional unavailability as well as difficulties with her siblings helped her to stop engaging in fantasy. Over time, she was able to see that all women have good and bad parts. Including herself.

No Porn or Masturbation

Some lesbians find themselves masturbating or using porn in destructive ways. For many, masturbating becomes an addiction causing the brain to develop a large tolerance to neurotransmitters, thereby requiring more porn—and sometimes hardcore porn—and more masturbation to satisfy the itch. If this is the case, stay away from these behaviors and from all porn until your system is healed and you are no longer physically addicted to it. Working with your therapist, sponsor, recovery buddy, or support system you can reintroduce these ways of experiencing pleasure if desired, but only when it is appropriate and you are ready to take this step. Some lesbians can return to porn without the fear of developing a tolerance or addiction to it; however, many cannot. It is easier for many recovering love addicts to reintegrate masturbation into their lives once the withdrawal period is over and overall healing has occurred.

Charley also put porn and masturbation on her bottom-line list because, as you know, this was her one of her drugs of choice. This was a very difficult step for Charley. For most of her life, she had relied on porn to numb her feelings and blunt the pain that her childhood trauma had caused. She slipped along the way, but she kept going to SLAA meetings, therapy, working with her sponsor on the twelve steps, and walking through her withdrawal process. She worked week to week then eventually went an entire month without intriguing, watching porn, or masturbating. Her next step was two months, and when she finally reached six months without porn, she celebrated. As her time away from her destructive behavior increased, her need for it was disappearing. Each month got easier and easier.

Money

For some love addicts, money issues play a part in their love addiction. Maybe you were the one who felt compelled to pay for everything because it built your self-worth, or perhaps you thought that money guarded you from being abandoned. If money is part of your addiction, your healing process should provide you with an opportunity to really look at any issues you have with money and how it relates to your self-worth. Doing so will help build a healthy foundation for when you begin dating again.

FOCUS ON HEALING YOUR LOVE ADDICTION

Thankfully, with some time and direct attention to your addiction, the withdrawal symptoms decrease. It does take time and a strong commitment to hold on to your bottom lines and not "act out" or engage in negative or destructive behavior. *Acting out* is a term used in the field of addiction to point out a return to addictive or self-destructive behavior.[13] When the love addict or love avoidant can stick to her agreed-upon bottom lines, she opens herself up to feeling calmer, more grounded, and more in control of her life.

WHAT IS YOUR BOTTOM LINE?

Recovering from this addiction is a subjective experience with rules that will vary from person to person. I encourage you to explore and create your bottom lines with your therapist, sponsor, or trusted recovery buddy instead of attempting to do it alone. To begin, I'd like to ask you to write a list after you finish reading this chapter. Taking this step doesn't require you to start doing any of it just yet, but it will help you to feel ready when you intentionally go into the withdrawal process, and it is a good idea to consider what your bottom lines would be, especially if they have not been covered in this book. I have included a bottom-line modified worksheet originally developed by Dr. David Bissette in figure 5-1 as a guide.[14] There are three categories often used in twelve-step self-help groups when becoming abstinent of certain behaviors that can really help you end your love-addicted behaviors for good.

Bottom-Line Behaviors

These are things you must absolutely not engage in. The activities fall into two categories—the ones that have created significantly negative consequences and losses: career, significant other, family, finances, legal, and health. They may include contacting your qualifier or sleeping with a woman outside of your committed relationship. The second category can cause you to spiral down or feel crazy. They cause you to obsess or lose your equanimity through activities such as texting, e-mailing, talking to an ex; engaging in euphoric recall; seducing women to feel validated; or going after unavailable women.

Middle-Line Behaviors

These are behaviors that you might engage in, but only with caution. Sometimes being too permissive with yourself can lead you back to square one. Middle lines have consequences that are hazy, such as fantasizing about your next partner, or saying yes when you mean no.

Matilda's middle-line behaviors included: don't hang with lesbians who party often; be careful of crushing on lesbians who party too much; watch for signs of trying to rescue anyone or controlling situations.

Top-Line Behaviors

These are considered healthy behaviors. They are encouraged because they are good for self-care. They can include therapy, meditation, exercise, being in nature, and engaging in creative activities such as art, poetry, music—anything that helps you access those creative parts of yourself. All of these should feel good, fun, and relaxing. We'll go over this guide in more detail in the next chapter. Please refer there for examples of what top lines are in order to help you formulate your own list.

WHAT HAPPENS WHEN YOU ARE WITHDRAWING?

Physiologically speaking, the brain and CNS are recovering from an overuse of the feel-good chemicals created by all the behaviors that released them. Over time, these chemicals have a negative impact on the body. Like all addictions, it takes more and more intense engage-

BOTTOM LINE WORKSHEET

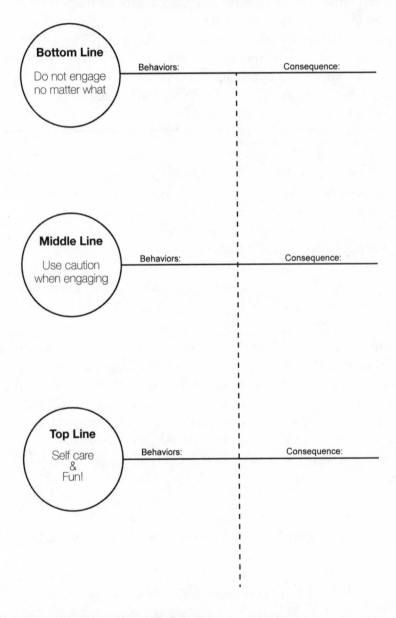

Figure 5.1.   The Bottom-Line Worksheet.

ment in the addictive behaviors for the desired result. Early in AA, the focus was on the progression of the "disease."[15] Although they did not have the science back then to back up their claims at that time, they saw what happened to alcoholics who didn't get sober increases in tolerance. Now we have the science to back up this theory. The brain quite literally needs more and more to feed the neurons. Taking from what we learned in previous chapters about the plasticity of the brain, repeatedly feeding neurons with a specific chemical wires the neurons to need more of that chemical to create the high. A pamphlet on withdrawal provided by SLAA provides a list of symptoms experienced when going through withdrawal. I have created a modified list of them here to help you understand what is happening once you embark on the withdrawal process:

- Cravings to act out on your love-addicted behaviors
- Inexplicable aches and pains
- Physical illness or exhaustion
- A switch to new addictions
- Changes in eating or sleeping patterns
- General self-doubt
- Desperation and fear
- Suicidal thoughts
- Desire to isolate
- Obsessive thinking
- Sadness, depression, or despair
- Fantasies about the behaviors or woman you gave up
- Emotional highs and lows
- Irritability, anger, or rage
- Confusion or trouble concentrating[16]

When Mary started dating after Tina, she had no idea her love addiction was getting worse. In fact, she thought it was better. She believed the intense and magical "love" she and Jane were experiencing meant that they were destined for each other. So while the initial merging with Jane made her high, it was still not enough. To sustain the same feeling, she demanded unlimited amounts of unconditional love. She needed the constant texting, unconditional positive regard, and the fantasy that they were to be together forever just to feel normal. When the merger started to shift, as it does in all relationships, her trauma was triggered. In the back of her mind were her mother and Tina's repeated rejections. Having Jane's desire reassured her that she was not going to get hurt. Initially their bond created a sense of safety Mary had been craving her whole life. "I am ok as long as I am not rejected or left—that is how I stay safe."

Knowing how the female brain works, this thinking makes complete sense. We are wired to need those we attach to for our very survival. But because Mary did not get that emotionally from her mother, this unmet childhood need haunted her as an adult lesbian. Her mother's ambivalent behavior created an insecure attachment in Mary. Whenever a girlfriend she loved rejected her she would experience intense, overwhelming pain.

To avoid pain, the brain will crave its drug. If this is not possible, withdrawal symptons start, such as agitation, anxiety, and depression. If love addiction has run its course, the brain cannot continue to produce the addictive chemicals anymore. Meaning the neurotransmitters need time to heal so that they can start creating their own chemicals again. Once the withdrawal period is over and the brain starts functioning at a normal level again, the hope is the brain will start emitting those feel-good chemicals in a balanced way. This is called homeostasis, the point at which the body and brain do not need to achieve this state.[17] This new adjusted level of dopamine and oxytocin isn't enough to create a high, but it can certainly help create feelings of well-being. If you don't feel better after a prolonged period and you are still feeling in danger for your safety, it is time to be evaluated by a medical professional. Together you can figure out what your brain and neurons might need to return to a balanced state.

There is a reason why the love addict is unable to stop herself from contacting the person she's become addicted to. Her ANS has been compromised. Because repeated exposure to her qualifier triggers a return to the injury, complete withdrawal from her is the first step in repairing the damage. Complete abstinence allows the nervous system to calm down and start regulating itself again. For some women abstinence is not enough to heal the pain. This is when support meetings, therapy, SLAA, trauma, and bodywork can be a great boon to the healing process.

In "Reward, Addiction, and Emotion Regulation Systems Associated with Rejection in Love," Fisher and her colleagues explain their research on addiction to the rejecting romantic partner:

> We predicted that rejected men and women would express neural activity in cortical and subcortical areas associated with craving and addiction when they viewed the rejecter relative to the neutral photograph, particularly the nucleus accumbens and orbitofrontal/ prefrontal cortex because our rejected participants reported that they thought about their rejecter obsessively and craved emotional union with their rejecting partner. Our prediction was supported.[18]

THE FIVE STAGES OF GRIEF

The idea that there existed a natural progression of grieving that humans go through when losing a loved one was first introduced by Elizabeth Kubler-Ross in 1969.[19] Examining what happens to people who experience the death of someone they knew, Kubler-Ross's insights about the emotional states or stages of grief that follow death have helped millions of people struggling with the painful emotions of this experience. As awareness of her theory of the cycles of grief grew, psychologists used Kubler-Ross's theories to explain the grieving process that happens when a relationship ends. Looking at breakups as a kind of death, these five stages have been adapted and applied to the separation process that couples experience.

Shock and Denial

The first stage of the grief process involves the initial feeling of shock experienced by the breakup, combined with attempts to deny or avoid the inevitable ending of the relationship. Most breakups that occur in lesbian love-addicted relationships, even for those who have been in the spiral for a while and appear to acknowledge or accept that the inevitable end is coming, go through the shock and denial phase. This is how the psyche protects itself from taking in the gravity of the situation too quickly. It is a very important protective mechanism. Soon the reality of the situation will sink in and the other phases will begin to unfold.

Anger

This phase can come on pretty fast after the shock dissipates, especially once the no contact boundary has been made. The kind of anger that occurs in this stage is different than the anger experienced in the spiral. Usually it involves feelings of rejection or betrayal, which can make it much more painful. In the spiral phase the idea that the relationship still holds some possibility, or that your partner will remain in your life, is still there. Once the reality hits, that you will never be with your loved one again, that she is still alive and breathing and may already be dating other women, the anger can be overwhelming. Maybe you made more money than your partner, and you paid for most things and now you regret having been so generous with her. Who made you angry, but perhaps never discussed, may arise now.

If a love avoidant broke your heart because she was emotionally and physically unavailable, unexpected anger may appear. Rejection and heartbreak have a way of igniting the opposite side of passion. It can have an obsessive quality to it, making you feel powerless to stop it. It is often tinged with fantasies or thoughts of revenge or inflicting harm. Don't worry, this is perfectly normal. This comes from the desire for your ex to hurt like you are hurting. The truth is, we can't really know or compare our pain, but this doesn't stop our minds from wondering if the excruciating pain we feel is shared. What we are doing is trying to make sense of the pain we feel. Experiencing pain on our own after sharing our pain with a partner can be unbearable. Acting on those fantasies of harm, of course, is not healthy. Beating down her door at three in the morning because you can't sleep—not a good idea.

Bargaining

While there are still tinges of anger surfacing, one way the addiction tries to alleviate them is to start imagining a way out. This is when the heart and mind move on to envisioning a reunion as the answer. For this to make any kind of sense, idealizing must occur. This is called *euphoric recall*, a phenomenon that often occurs when one is in the throes of withdrawal.[20] This happens when the love addict idealizes her ex or their relationship, to the extent that she completely forgets the negative aspects of their relationship. During this time one is most vulnerable to relapse or returning to the ex. Not surprisingly, many women find fantasizing about the good times provides not only relief but also a "hit" from their favorite chemicals—dopamine and oxytocin. This is because the fantasy itself can cause these chemicals to be released, thereby starting an avalanche of regret, "Oh no, did I make a mistake?" Matilda would ask me. "No," I would answer, "remember what the relationship was really like." It can become more of a tease than anything else because the good feelings that return are not enough to satisfy the craving, and soon the unhealthy behavior is reignited. This is often when two women will get back together despite knowing the relationship is unhealthy. So this is when bottom lines come in handy. Having these established boundaries with yourself are often what prevents unnecessary contact with an ex, intriguing with a coworker, or flirting at a bar over the weekend.

During the early stages of Josie's withdrawal, she had many euphoric recall episodes of Danielle. She struggled with the urge to drive by Danielle's home, which would give her the hit she required. Although Danielle had betrayed her, that betrayal would conveniently slip her mind during these moments. For months, she would come into therapy remembering only how good Danielle had made her feel. She would reminisce about the hot sex and wistfully think about their intense connection. While this was an important part of her process, to think about Danielle in order to get over her, it was an equally important part of my job to help her remember all of Danielle, as opposed to just the one Josie's addiction wanted her to remember. Danielle was not a bad person, and it was not my intention to demonize her, but I did want Josie to remember that Danielle had not only gotten involved with her while she was still married to her ex-wife but that she had also become less available once her marriage ended. I had to repeatedly help Josie remember that Danielle had left her for their band's drummer, while they were still officially dating. Josie would leave each session grateful that I had reminded her of these details, which she repeatedly "forgot."

In addiction, obsession can be one of the most personally and emotionally damaging symptoms. For lesbian love addicts, euphoric recall or obsession of the ex-girlfriend is a very difficult part of the withdrawal process. The lesbian love-addicted brain is prone to obsessively thinking about the person who helped them get high and temporarily assuaged their attachment issues. Shifting away from that behavior can be challenging and often the reason a woman will return to her ex, even when the relationship does not work.

Depression

It is common to go through bouts of depression when you are grieving the loss of a relationship. We all know how hard it is to let go of someone you love, and the pain of having your heart broken is excruciating. When the shock, denial, anger, and bargaining subside, depression is usually next. It means that you are accepting the situation, moving through the sadness of the loss, and getting prepared to live your life without your ex.

Just as she withdrew from Danielle and her love-addicted behavior ceased, Josie consciously experienced her first depressive episode. It took her by surprise. She felt sad, alone, scared, and robbed of energy. More days than not she cried, and she spent much of our sessions together crying. Around this time Josie began to focus her energy on me. At the end of one of our sessions, she asked me out to dinner. On another occasion, she asked me to sit next to her on the couch. Finally, Josie revealed she had always had a crush on me. The psychological term for this experience of developing romantic and sexual feelings toward a therapist is *erotic transference*. With both her marriage and her love-addicted relationship ending, Josie's fearful response was to turn her charm onto me. Her felt experience of asking me out or suggesting that we kiss provided a moment when her depression lifted and she felt ogod.

Establishing a safe environment for Josie to work out her myriad of feelings for me, educating her about erotic transference, and assuring her that I would never break the sanctity of our therapeutic boundaries by giving into her wishes allowed Josie the opportunity to delve into the depths of her grief, which went much deeper than her wife and Danielle. This led us to her relationship with her mother. Her mother, while loving and kind, was inherently narcissistic. Josie was confusing the love she had for her unavailable mother, who was unable to meet her needs emotionally while growing up, with the feelings she developed while in my care. It is very common in lesbian love addiction for women to confuse care, concern, and consistency with romantic love, if that kind of love was missing from their relationship with their mothers during those important developmental years. Not getting the love she deserved had created a feeling of emptiness in Josie that she used her romantic life to fix. Seeing the traits of her mother's narcissism clearly and understanding the immense unmet need still inside her was a difficult set of truths to digest. The more we talked about and explored these deficits in her childhood, the greater her relief. It made sense. Once she could see and experience the real issues underlying her need to romanticize our relationship or go after unavailable women, she began to feel more hope about the healing process. Eventually, I steered her toward several books on narcissistic parenting. One in particular that was very helpful to her was Dr. Karyl McBride's *Will I Ever Be Good Enough? Healing the Daughters of Narcissistic Mothers*, which I recommend if you relate to any of these stories.

Acceptance

Acceptance happens when your psyche has truly taken in the reality of the situation. Acceptance is a stage of release when you no longer feel the need for things to be different from how they are. In fact, this is when many lesbians finally experience the emotional freedom that comes from leaving a toxic relationship.

MEANING THROUGH THE GRIEF

Let's take a moment to focus on what we get, rather than what we lose, as we separate from the past. If we allow ourselves to move through the grieving process with an open heart and mind, the possibility of finding meaning through our suffering presents itself. Yes, this seems impossible to do while we are in the throes of suffering, especially when grieving not only the loss of a loved one but healing a broken heart, in addition to the many other problems your love addiction may have caused you. It is a lot to bear, and for many it is almost too much to endure. This is precisely why love addiction is one of the most uncomfortable and difficult addictions to overcome, and why so many of us deny it for years, until denial stops working.

The SLAA program is smaller than many of the other twelve-step programs. Many who attend have a difficult time staying mainly because withdrawal can be so difficult. In my practice, I have seen many clients deny their love addiction for years. The cost of avoiding the painful truth is being in a nonstop cycle of excruciating relationships. Many are inclined to suffer rather than face the addiction and go through the withdrawal process because it is such an unknown and frightening territory.

That said, when the grief and withdrawal are finally over, the rewards are plenty. Not only have you survived the tremendously empowering process of giving up behaviors that were threatening your future health and happiness, you also let go of a toxic relationship. Perhaps more important, you began the process of healing your childhood and societal trauma attachment issues. None of this could be done without first facing the issues head on. No small feat.

Second, without the love-addicted behaviors medicating your childhood issues and keeping you stuck and distracted by the merger trap and lesbian love addiction spiral, you have opened yourself up to deeper insight and new levels of consciousness. This is when the real healing begins. Many lesbians who have gone through this process report that once they reach the other side of grieving and withdrawal, it was worth all the effort. Just as the founder of SLAA suggested, withdrawal is a precious time, even when it is impossible to appreciate that until it is behind you. Most can't say enough about the lightness they start to feel once they've detoxified from this addiction and become free from its grip. We'll delve into this in more detail in the next chapter.

SLIPS VERSUS RELAPSES

Slips

A slip is considered a temporary return to the addictive behavior. It may happen only one time, or in one deluded thought, or it can last for a few days. Slips are not considered disasters because they are short-lived. Let me be clear. I do not encourage slips, but they can happen, and when they do, being judged or criticized by others (or yourself) is not helpful. Often a slip is the exact lesson an addict needs to confirm her inability to "just have a little." Slips provide momentary relief, which everyone is seeking, but they are usually followed by feelings of regret. Ideally a slip experience will lead the addict to a revelation about an unhealthy behavior or person, and this awareness helps the addict let go and embrace healing. On the road to recovery from love addiction, these slips are normal, and for some, necessary. At the very least, we can applaud their short lifetime. The other good news about a slip is that it is not a relapse. A full-blown relapse, as Mary's return to her love addiction was, is a prolonged return to the old destructive and unconscious behaviors.

About a year after Charley's marriage ended, she found her way to SLAA meetings. A successful AAer, she loved the twelve steps and was confident this program could help her, just as AA had helped her get sober from alcoholism. But Charley was not prepared for the withdrawal she experienced with this addiction. Fortunately, she had a sponsor and over time set her bottom lines: no contact or intriguing with any woman at work, no flirting, no sexting, no porn, no masturbation to porn, and no contact with her last sex partner. Charley was excited to get sober from this addiction and move on with her life, but maintaining sobriety proved to be much harder than she could have ever imagined. Immediately, she became vulnerable to slips. As she grew more restless and agitated, she found herself euphorically recalling her qualifier, and eventually she found it impossible to stay away from her. This grew into texting her, which turned into sexting her. The good news is she stopped there. Though she was tempted to hook up with her, she did not. Instead, she called her sponsor and upped her meeting schedule. She eventually stopped contacting her qualifier and got back to her bottom lines. Of course, the withdrawal returned. When she found it unbearable, she watched porn. And so it went. It took Charley about six months before she obtained ninety days of sticking to her bottom lines. The ninetieth day was a big day for Charley, and she has not looked back since. During those ninety successful days, Charley also decided to attend lesbian-affirmative therapy. This is when she realized that her sexual trauma would continue to have an impact on her and any future relationships if she didn't heal this part of her history.

Relapse

A relapse is more destructive than a slip because it signals a return to the former addictive behavior, even after experiencing the benefits of clarity, sobriety, and recovery. It also signifies a return to a denial of the problem as we saw when Mary left SLAA and returned to her love addiction. Relapse often involves an increase in the former behaviors for two reasons. First, the addiction intensifies because the brain's tolerance to the high increases. Second, the psychological issues influencing the addiction remain untreated, and this fuels the need to medicate the trauma that is behind the addiction.

HEALING THE TRAUMA

Both the love addict and love avoidant will find giving attention to their traumas—those issues that are often the source the addiction—helpful during recovery. Devoting time and energy to examine attachment traumas, familial issues, conflicts with friends, or simply the trauma of living in a heterocentric and lesbianphobic society will help heal the withdrawal period. By addressing these issues from a lesbian-affirmative perspective and a thorough understanding of love addiction and how to work with trauma in a way that addresses the CNS can help release you from the trap of addiction. Addressing addiction's underlying issues provides context and meaning, a deeper understanding of the source of addiction, and clarity about the withdrawal process. Encouraging lesbians to be accountable for the state of their lives and empowering them toward the wholeness and the well-being that every person is inherently capable of is an important part of this experience. In the next chapter we'll go over a few trauma-based techniques that focus on healing the ANS specifically. They have been found to be very effective in aiding the recovery process.

WHAT'S NEXT?

Now that you know more about withdrawal and the commitment and patience it requires, don't be surprised if you find yourself resisting it. This fear is natural. How could you not be at least a little bit cautious? This is a big and courageous step to take. Getting started can be the hardest part, but it is also the gateway to liberation. I cannot emphasize enough how important this part of your healing process is, and how effective it is in helping you find happiness and wholeness in your life.

Once you clear the hurdle of withdrawal, the strength and awareness you will gain will follow you throughout your life. Mary describes it best:

> I thought the hardest thing I ever went through was losing my mom until I went through withdrawal from my love addiction. My mom's death was quick and unexpected. She was healthy until she was diagnosed with cancer and then gone a month later. I thought I was going crazy during that experience but nothing prepared me for withdrawing from Jane and my love addiction. During withdrawal I also thought I was going crazy, but I didn't see an end in sight and I could not find meaning in my pain, which made the entire situation seem pointless. When my mom was dying, as a spiritual person I knew I would recover one day, I knew she was going to be ok and I knew I would find some meaning in her loss. It was not until I celebrated my first year of recovery from love addiction that I began to see the meaning in it all. I began to feel lighter. After a while, I not only felt better, I had freed myself from using love and other women to medicate how I felt about myself. I know that developing a healthy sense of self is an ongoing process, but when I stopped engaging in my love addiction my life really turned around.

The next chapter will highlight the different ways to develop a healthy and loving relationship with yourself and others, which is the final stage in healing from lesbian love addiction.

6

HOW TO HAVE A HEALTHY RELATIONSHIP WITH YOURSELF AND OTHERS

Your vision will become clear only when you can look into your own heart. Who looks outside, dreams; who looks inside, awakens.

—C. G. Jung[1]

Congratulations are in order. Throughout the course of reading this book, you've made a great deal of progress. First, by becoming aware of the unique challenges that befall lesbian love addiction, and then by learning about the steps that are necessary for withdrawal and sobriety. Now you are ready to restart your life and reconnect with the healthy, happy, playful you! This starts with learning some of the practical techniques of self-care. By establishing a new—and well-earned—routine that replaces unhealthy and painful behaviors with self-respect and self-compassion you are choosing to heal and to grow. In SLAA terms, you are connecting to your own unique top-line behaviors.[2] We'll go over a number of them, and soon you will be on your way to enhanced self-esteem and a stronger understanding of your own worth. The goal is pretty simple when you think about it. With your newly heightened awareness, you are ready to do the work it takes to finally attract a healthy and sustainable romantic relationship that is free of addictive behaviors. My hope is that the following tips can serve as a guide toward greater happiness and satisfaction in all areas of your life.

CONNECTING WITH YOURSELF

From time to time you might ask yourself—*what am I doing all of this inner work for?* I want you to have some answers to this difficult basic question ready and waiting should you need it. Remember, if we peel away all the layers of lesbian love addiction, what we find is an intimacy disorder. The urge to merge is a real problem for many lesbians, and perhaps for you too. But you can heal and choose to see love addiction as an obstacle rather than an irreparable problem. Learning to be intimate in the face of this obstacle will change your life. As lesbians and as women we are neurologically wired to connect to other women, and overcoming the challenges we face when we become unbalanced in this area of our lives can be very distressing.

Healthy relationships bring meaning and fulfillment to our lives.[3] As you begin to recover from lesbian love addiction, you should see and experience all the good things that open up to you as a result of this shift. The first of these is having the opportunity to connect with yourself. Before you can figure out how to have a healthy and truly fulfilling connection with another woman, you must learn more about what it means to be your authentic self. Having this time to get to know who you really are, and what really makes you tick, is a great opportunity that will have a profound effect on the rest of your life. Understanding what it means to live as your authentic self is not just an invaluable gift to yourself, it is also the means by which you can have a healthy relationship with another person, or recommit to the one you are already connected to. So moving forward, recognize that by embracing your authentic self you will discover new ways to make your life the best it can be, and in doing so, you will be ready to share yourself with someone else.

THE HEROINE'S JOURNEY

Joseph Campbell calls it *The Hero's Journey*. This is the process of getting in touch with your inner world, finding your true calling, and creating meaning that feels authentic to you.[4] As lesbians who are committed to the work of discovering ourselves, we won't be using male-centric terms, so for our purposes we'll call it "The Heroine's Journey."

Fellow heroines take note: You have taken the essential first steps, you have discovered an addiction, which keeps you living in an illusion, and you have been brave enough to step outside of that addiction. What is that illusion? It is the fantasy that keeps you acting on your lesbian love addiction that sucks you into its spiral and watches as you repeat, year after year, decade upon decade, one unhealthy experience after another. The illusion that you will finally find meaning and the one true perfect love if only you could meet the right woman keeps you from creating a healthy relationship. The reality is, love addiction has kept you stuck in painful and self-destructive patterns with yourself and others, and you will not come close to attracting authentic love until you break that pattern.

Waking up from an addiction is like waking up from a deep sleep. For some it includes major *a-ha* moments like we saw with Mary. For others, the awareness might not be quite as instantaneous. The intensity may feel more like a slow burn, but either way the results are the same. Waking up is really a call to ignore the delusions of your addiction and find who you truly are. Campbell talks about it as a call from deep inside yourself—that soulful, spirited place inside each of us that craves meaning, love, adventures, health, and satisfying relationships. It is this place inside, inside all human beings, where our essence, that feeling of being alive and creating our own destiny, is held. At some point in all of our lives we are asked to hear and acknowledge this call. Not all people listen to it, but if you are reading this book then your ears are open and you are ready to hear it. Whether you already had a rewarding a-ha moment, or the insights and understandings are trickling in more slowly, the good news is that you have arrived at this point. You are on your way to developing a more meaningful relationship with yourself that can lead to an amazing life.

It is called the Heroine's Journey because you are becoming the heroine of your own life. There is no one else who can do this work for you, and it is entirely up to you to make it happen. It takes a lot of courage to face your demons and jump into the unknown, but since you are the heroine, I am confident that you can do it. You would not be reading this book if you had not already been called to wake up and find yourself. How exciting! As scary as it can be, I bet there are parts of you that are exhilarated and thrilled to have this opportunity to change your life for the better.

Some of the power of addiction comes from the ease and familiarity it generates. Like any habit, it is something you've come to rely upon. I'd bet your love addiction feels very satisfying in some ways. It's most likely brought you many euphoric moments throughout your life. There is almost a sense of comfort in its recklessness. This is because, like all habitual behaviors, it becomes second nature to you. Much of it is based in our biology, which you know has a very strong pull on us. But the problem with these easy and familiar feelings is that they don't last. They are neither sustainable nor reliable. But you now have the opportunity to start creating a secure attachment with yourself that will last a lifetime. By creating a secure attachment, healing those neuronal pathways that were damaged by your trauma and addictions, developing healthy coping mechanisms and a regimen of self-care, you have the chance to create the life you have always envisioned for yourself.

TAKING THE RED PILL

The first film in *The Matrix* trilogy (which was co-created by Lana Wachowski, an out lesbian transwoman), the straight, male protagonist Neo is called upon to wake up and help his fellow humans. He is tasked with guiding other humans out of the false system that keeps them stuck in the primary delusion of life. Neo is given the opportunity by his mentor, Morpheus, to either take the red pill that will take him out of the Matrix forever or take the blue pill that will bring him back into his cocoon where he will continue to sleep. Neo decides to take the red pill and leave the Matrix.[5]

The film shows us the difficulties faced by those who leave the Matrix. If we look at this story—and Neo's dilemma—through the lens of addiction, we can see that Neo's struggle parallels the struggle many of us face to get sober. Neo experiences symptoms of withdrawal, and undergoing physical recovery from life out of the Matrix proves to be a difficult and uncomfortable experience, not unlike the process of recovering from love addiction. There are many painful, even frightening moments, which Neo must endure in his rigorous training to become his true self. He learns to master the skill of fighting through a journey filled with falls and mistakes. In the end, though, Neo becomes the master of his life—"enlightened" so to speak.

I encourage you to use Neo's story for inspiration and to see it as analogous to the healing parts of your journey. Consider all you've been through, what it took to get you here, and see this as an opportunity for you to decide what kind of therapy will help you heal best—whether you might benefit from SLAA or another twelve-step program, or start a meditation practice, or some other type of spiritual program that can guide you to a deeper state of awareness. In learning to practice self-compassion, give yourself the time and the space to explore what's inside of you, and go deep within to find out who you really are. This might be a good time to slow down your life instead of filling up all your time with activities or people. Let's look at many of the psychological self-care techniques you might want to employ to help you get there.

PSYCHOLOGICAL SELF-CARE

Traditional Psychotherapy, Known as Talk Therapy

Psychotherapy has been around for more than a century now, and thankfully the stigma around it is mostly behind us. Having a therapist isn't something to be ashamed of, nor do we or fear it makes us seem "crazy." If you live in a community where shameful attitudes and ignorance about psychotherapy exists, I strongly urge you to ignore those uniformed opinions. Therapy helps millions of people every day. I am not saying this because I am a therapist. I have also been a client for many years, and I have experienced the benefits of psychotherapy. In fact, I could not have taken my own red pill, and woken up from my own delusions about love addiction without the help of my therapists over the years.

When choosing a therapist, there are several basic questions you must ask. The first and foremost question is, does the therapist feel like a great fit for you? Just because your best friend highly recommended someone, you shouldn't feel obligated. It is imperative you find the right person for you. Maybe your friend's therapist, or someone you trust, can make a recommendation for you. Also, ask if your therapist knows about trauma, addiction, and finally, are they lesbian-affirmative—or is at least willing to learn what lesbian-affirmative psychotherapy is. These therapeutic specialties can bridge gaps in understanding and will help make your recovery from lesbian love addiction more effective.

Therapy is a place to be yourself—warts and all. A good therapist is a natural empath and should create an environment in which you feel encouraged to be authentic. He or she will be nonjudgmental, compassionate, knowledgeable, competent, and licensed in their field. Ideally, the therapist you choose is kind but firm. You don't want someone who can't recognize or is afraid to call you out on your acting-out behavior. A great therapist will help you see when you are caught up in shame, guilt, or delusion, and point out when you are behaving in ways that are sabotaging, addictive, and ultimately self-harming. Being emotionally vulnerable with a stranger is difficult for some people at first. It might even feel strange and very unfamiliar to disclose thoughts and feelings you have always kept secret, but it will get easier if you open up and let yourself.

While in therapy, pay attention to those parts of you that feel shameful. It is completely normal to experience feelings of shame, but avoiding or denying them will not help you heal. In fact, it may keep you stuck. Now that you are no longer in denial about your love addiction, or confused about your level of addiction, you have the opportunity to dive into this work with the guidance of a professional who is objective and cares about your well-being. Do it—you deserve it.

Don't let expense deter you from healing. If you are on a tight budget, reach out to a local psychotherapy clinic. You can find a sliding-scale intern who has a good supervisor helping them with their cases. If you have a local LGBTQ center, call them and ask them to help you find the right person at the right price. Remember, your anonymity is always of utmost importance to a professional psychotherapist, so be yourself and get the most out of the experience.

Benefits of Talk Psychotherapy

Those of us who have self-esteem and self-worth challenges have a well-developed inner critic.[6] You've learned in the previous chapters how our brains are naturally wired to worry and how growing up in a hetero-centric and lesbianphobic world can create low self-esteem in lesbians. This can leave us with a powerful inner critic. Therapy helps with this in many ways. First, with the aid of this book, you can stop blaming, shaming, or guilting yourself for being a love addict. By now you can see how it is not your fault.

You are not a love addict because something is inherently wrong with you—that is the toxic shame and lesbianphobia talking. Those harmful voices want you to believe you could have done more to prevent your problems, but this is simply not true. The powerful motives of our inner critics are complex, and the messages they send us are often cruel, relentless, and manipulative. A good therapist can help you stop believing them. He or she will recognize when you are colluding with these critical voices and point out how they impact you. Remember, awareness and understanding can disempower the inner critic. There are good workbooks you can find to help deepen this process as you go along. While heterocentric in nature, I still recommend *The Illustrated Workbook for Self-Therapy for Your Inner Critic* by social worker Bonnie Weiss.[7] If you are finding your inner critic to be particularly problematic, these kinds of workbooks can be a great aid in your work with your therapist.

Recognizing that you have been victimized by ruthlessly shaming societal structures can help you distance yourself from them. I am not promulgating a victim mentality here. The opposite of that is true. You have been victimized, but you are a survivor who is extremely courageous, and you are here because you are ready to heal the lies you have been taught. With this work, your inner critic, internalized lesbianphobia, and toxic shame will lose their power over time.

TRAUMA-BASED THERAPY MODALITIES

There are a number of trauma-based therapies out there, and I recommend two of them as ways to enhance your healing process.

Trauma Resilience Model

The Trauma Resilience Model (TRM)[8] created by Elaine Miller-Karas, Laurie Leitch, and Geneie Everett is specifically geared toward healing the CNS and ANS affected by trauma. Focusing on what they coined "the resilient zone," that place inside the CNS that experiences well-being, confidence, excitement, happiness, and a sense of calm, a trained

TRM therapist or community leader will teach you how to access your resilient zone while thinking or talking about painful and traumatic experiences. This allows the ANS to release and heal any stuck trauma while at the same time helping the client create ways to access their resilient zone whenever necessary. For more information, please go to http://traumaresourceinstitute.com/trauma-resiliency-model-trm/.

Eye Movement Desensitization and Reprocessing Therapy

Around for decades, Eye Movement Desensitization and Reprocessing Therapy (EMDR) is an evidence-based practice that uses "dual stimulation" in which toning, tapping, or eye movements, all external stimuli, are utilized while the client recounts past traumas or future worries. This often produces insights or new memories around issues needing healing.[9] For more information, please go to http://www.emdr.com/general-information/what-is-emdr.html.

Self-Compassion

This is where working to tame your inner critic really comes in handy. Replacing your inner critic with compassion is effective. If you did not receive much compassion from your mother, father, or siblings and were therefore unable to internalize a kind, loving voice, this is a challenge, but it is definitely doable. The idea of compassion is thoroughly explored in *The Art of Happiness*, which psychiatrist Howard Cutler cowrote with His Holiness, the Dalai Lama. This book is a great resource for understanding compassion as a state of mind.[10] Developing compassion for yourself starts with the wish to be free of suffering and dissatisfaction. Genuine compassion for all beings comes from the wish that everyone can be happy and free of suffering. These two sides of suffering can help us remember that struggle is part of the human condition, but everyone—including you—has an innate desire and ability to be fundamentally happy and free of suffering. We will count on those parts as you delve further into this chapter.

In learning to generate self-compassion, many people find that perfectionism stands in the way. Start by asking yourself if you feel that you need to be perfect to be loved. Accepting that all humans are imperfect is an important part of creating compassion for yourself. When you make a mistake, remind yourself how normal that is. Everyone makes mistakes. When you are feeling vulnerable and sad, remember that everyone deals with sadness and pain. You are not alone when it comes to facing difficult things in your life.

Engaging in work around your childhood trauma is another imperative to healing. So often we forget that we were once open, vulnerable, and genuine as children. Watch children at play and imagine yourself at two, three, and five years of age. Remember that you were that age once, with all your innocence and vulnerability still intact. Remember how much you relied on, looked up to, and loved your mother and other important adult figures. Think about what might have happened to those innocent parts of you if you were neglected, shamed, abused, or if you grew up in an addictive or unconscious home. Think about how hard that must have been on your inner little girl, and give her some love. She deserves it, and you will be grateful you started doing it.

Our Shadow

Developing compassion also means embracing and forgiving yourself for having darker parts to your psyche. In Jungian psychology, we call these parts our shadow. We all have one, and we were all born with them. Children are also wired to be selfish and demanding. They can't help themselves. Developmentally speaking, this is normal behavior, and it is our parents' and teachers' job to teach us how to manage those parts. It's not healthy to be a thirty-year-old who has temper tantrums. Of course we have all experienced *losing it* at some point in our adult lives. We are all prone to these kinds of childish behaviors, especially when in the throes of the lesbian love addiction spiral. This part of our inner work means we have to grow up and take responsibility for those childlike parts of us that are not nice, kind, or helpful. We all have them, and society could not manage if we didn't learn how to control them. But shaming them does not help you deal with them; it only leads to repressing them. Compassionately allowing them to exist inside of us is what heals us.

Buddhist nun and author Pema Chodron's *Getting Unstuck: Breaking Your Habitual Patterns and Encountering Naked Reality* is an effective guide for helping us watch the "uglier" parts of ourselves with curiosity and treat them nonjudgmentally.[11] By shaming those parts of ourselves we don't like, they go right back into their shell only to come out when we least expect or want them to. It is more helpful to give them attention in your inner work so that you can avoid directing them at others in more harmful ways. Maybe they represent those unmet needs you have never known how to ask for. Maybe they are the anger you feel toward aspects of your childhood. Maybe it is the guilt you feel for being angry. Maybe they represent the jealousy you have for some of your siblings who got more attention than you did. For lesbian love addicts, they are often those parts of us that had to deal with a hetero-centric and lesbianphobic world, but didn't want to see. If we invite them into our awareness, we get the opportunity to understand their origins. We can ask them why they feel injured and what they need to heal. Many of us have been rejected, hurt, misunderstood, or aban-doned, leaving us with feelings that are intolerable and hard to live with, feelings we are wired to avoid at all cost. But I am here to tell you as a therapist who works with people who have spent many years avoiding their feelings that it doesn't work. It is only when we make ourselves vulnerable and learn how to surrender to these parts of ourselves that we disempower them.

I will also tell you that facing these parts of yourself is no small or easy feat. However, this kind of inner work builds compassion and helps grow self-esteem. When you stop beating yourself up, you stop beating others up. You learn to embrace everyone's humanness, especially your own, and great relief can come from that. Embracing our limitations and shadowy parts enables us to step out of the pain that seems to own us. In her book *Daring Greatly: How the Courage to Be Vulnerable Transforms the Way We Live, Love, Parent and Lead*, Dr. Brené Brown provides many great lessons about the power of vulnerability. Brown's research shows that learning how to be vulnerable is the key to unlocking emotional freedom and happiness.[12] Leaning how to be vul-nerable with those we deem safe is also the secret to creating authentic intimacy with yourself and others.

Another interesting side to our shadow is that it also holds our po-tential and our most authentic self.[13] When we pushed away those parts of ourselves that our parents and society would not tolerate, such as our lesbianism, or our independent spirit, we had to push good parts away as well. Our parents and society may not have appreciated those qual-ities or truths in us, but they are vital to who we are. Perhaps they disliked our leadership qualities (too often girls are labeled "bossy," but this quality is encouraged in boys),[14] so we responded by making ourselves smaller.[15] Unfortunately, the parts of ourselves that are luminous, radiant, and full of promise are often put into our shadow as well. You have already started diving into your shadow by reading this book, engaging in lesbian-affirmative psychotherapy, learning about lesbianphobia and internalized lesbianphobia, healing your love addiction, and doing trauma work. This means you are already facing and embracing your shadow. So be forewarned, this could very well lead to levels of internal liberation you did not imagine were possible. Each time you work on these parts of yourself, you loosen up and release repressed energy taken up by the trauma in your psyche. Healing allows much of it to be released, and self-esteem, self-worth, and self-love start to emerge. It can be a wonderful, magical process.

Finding Your Voice

Remember that pesky amygdala and worry center? Remember how most of us are wired to keep the peace and avoid conflict? Add to that the trauma many of us have experienced and what you have is the nature meets nurture syndrome. Because our voices have been muted, we are afraid to state our needs, or ask for what we want, or express our feelings. Without a healthy voice or sense of self, our needs, feelings, and wants will come second to others. How do you feel good about yourself and believe you are worthy of a happy life if you never listened to your voice? Maybe you have swung in the opposite direction, being told that you are t considerate of others' feelings or you are too pushy when it comes to getting your way. Perhaps you have found that people shy away from you, or worse, eventually leave because of your *demands*, which are really based in your inability to ask for your needs to be met in a way that gels well with others. Both of these scenarios illustrate the behavior people whose voices were muted display. When we are not allowed to get our needs met in a healthy way, some of us respond in ways that look self-serving, which pushes away people we care about. Learning how to state our needs kindly and firmly while also knowing how to make healthy compromises, like letting your friend pick the restaurant or movie this time, can take some practice. Your therapist and outside support groups, can help you learn how to do this.

The key is to build these skills incrementally and to practice little by little. For example, if you have a friend who always picks the restaurant, state firmly what you want the next time you meet. If she balks, hold firm and say this is important to you. It might not sound like much, but building a strong, authentic voice is learned by trying the small things first. The more you do it, the easier it will get. Before you know it, honoring your own instincts and desires will become a habit. Ask for support if you are struggling with how to do this. Seek friends who know how to get their needs met and ask them how they figured it out.

TWELVE-STEP PROGRAMS

Finding SLAA, codependents anonymous, or other community-based recovery groups may take some time and work on your part. As I've mentioned, these groups are still in their infancy compared to other twelve-step programs that have been going strong for years. You may find love addiction groups more accessible in urban areas and cities. The good news is that now there are phone or teletherapy meetings. If a twelve-step program resonates with you but there are no SLAA meetings near you, go online to their main website, http://www.slaafws.org, and locate the women's phone meetings there.

If you are unsure about twelve-step programs because you are not comfortable with the religious or spiritual dimension, you are not alone. Many people share that discomfort but have found ways to get around that aspect and still benefit from meetings. Some people change the pronoun of the higher power from "he" to "she" or "he" to "it." SLAA is more sensitive to this issue and has substituted higher power for God in their twelve steps. Many programs have developed ways so that you don't have to be profoundly spiritual or religious to get something out of the program.

Another important benefit to twelve-step programs is finding other women like yourself who are struggling with this addiction and are finding ways to stay sober. Creating a recovery community will help you feel less alone, and meetings can be tremendously helpful when you are going through the withdrawal period. In this program, you can find a sponsor or recovery partners, women who will help you navigate the program and be there for you when you are having a hard day. [16] Recovery can be full of emotional ups and downs, and it is very helpful to have someone to call when, for instance, you inadvertently see your qualifier on a social media site and find yourself triggered and derailed by the experience. You do not have to do any of this alone. Talking to someone else, including your therapist, will help you move through this phase without having to break recovery by contacting the qualifier and having to start all over again. Processing our feelings not only makes us feel less alone; it helps us feel much better. As women we are wired to respond to and talk through our feelings and triggers, this is something that is powerful to embrace rather than deny and avoid.

COMMUNITY-BASED RECOVERY GROUPS

Spiritual or religious groups (non-lesbianphobic) such as Buddhist groups and spiritually based addiction groups, as well as LGBTQ center meetings and support groups are all helpful in creating communities that are focused on healing. Sometimes when a relationship ends we lose more than an ex-girlfriend, we can lose parts or all of our social circle and community. Her life and her friends became your life and your friends, and now that she is gone, you might need to meet new people who don't have anything to do with her, at least while you are healing. This is a healthy response. However, lesbian communities can be small, and this reality can make it particularly challenging to regroup and find a new set of friends. Community groups outside of your social circle offer a great opportunity to meet new people who are interested in growing and are on a similar path as you. Imagine the kinds of friends you can find now. Lastly, I am not suggesting you never be friends with your ex again. One of the wonderful parts of our community is that our ex's often become a close friend or part of our chosen family. It will depend on how destructive the relationship was. This is something you can go over with your therapist, sponsor, group counselor, and recovery buddies to figure out what is best for you and your recovery.

That said, be judicious during the initial stages of your recovery. We have to watch that love addiction tendency to want to jump in and belong to something quickly, especially those who are prone to that. Being flexible and open to new adventures is great, but if doing so without caution has caused problems in the past, remember to take time to get to know your new friends before giving them your all. If you are more of the guarded type, I am going to suggest you stretch yourself the other way. Go to meetings and join others for coffee or a meal afterward. But remember, don't start asking women you find attractive to coffee. This is not dating!

Mary handled this challenge by only approaching straight women for new friendships. She continued her lesbian friendships that involved zero attraction since she did not want to take any chances in the beginning. Because she was the type to jump in headfirst and ask questions later, she protected herself by playing it extra safe. Matilda was advised to do the opposite. As a guarded introvert, she had to push herself to meet new people. She befriended women she was not attracted to and started to develop a nice group of friends who were into creating more healthy lifestyles and similar in age.

JOURNALING

An ancient practice, journaling has helped many people throughout the ages.[17] It began during the time we lived in caves and we recorded our stories through pictures. Our psyches are naturally drawn to the healing aspects of telling our narrative, especially when we know it is for our eyes only. Journaling can really help us heal from lesbian love addition. This can be such a difficult journey at first, treacherous in fact, and writing down our thoughts is a great way to work through them.

GRATITUDE

Another form of journaling is writing down a list of all the things you feel thankful for. Doing this every night before you go to sleep is even better. This practice can be extremely helpful and self-esteem building. When we are in a lot of pain during the healing process, we need to focus on the trauma and pain to get through it, but even when we are in the throes of so much feeling, it is crucial to find balance. By reminding ourselves of the things we do have, and all that we are thankful for, we remind ourselves that devastating events do not prevent the good things from existing in our lives—your home, your pet, your job, your friends, the bird outside your window who chirps every morning. Choose to recognize that there is balance in your world.

PHYSICAL ACTIVITY

Exercise and conscious movement not only help us stay in touch with our bodies, they also release healthy feel-good chemicals called endorphins. As they interact with receptors in your brain, endorphins help create an energizing, positive attitude and can work like an analgesic to help reduce pain. If you are having a hard time moving because you feel depressed or you have health issues, bring exercise into your daily routine gradually. Start with a ten-minute walk or a few laps around the block before you start planning your marathon. Don't set yourself up for failure or injury by doing too much too soon. The more gradual success you achieve, the more you'll want to move around to keep the feeling. Try out new forms of exercise, and find something you like, something you can do even when you don't want to do it. Our bodies need to move around and release endorphins, which helps combat stress and improves sleep. We were never meant to sit as much as most of us do in the twenty-first century.

Consider yoga, spin classes, or walking in nature. Yoga was designed to shape the body into positions that help blood flow, energy, and muscle tone. If you are already into vigorous exercise, try something slower and see how relaxing it can be. Restorative yoga can help the parasympathic system do its job. Through gentle and long stretches your body has a chance to release pent-up cortisol and move your energy in a way that is invigorating. You'll notice that it's easier to relax when your body has been able to move and release cortisol and energy.

NATURE

Being in nature is incredibly healing. Eckhart Tolle's website features a great video about how powerful nature is for our souls. He describes how much easier it is to get into the present when in nature.[18] Our biological systems know how to attune to nature's frequency. Hiking, walking outside, going to the beach, and gardening—all of these activities give you the opportunity to be with yourself. They are wonderful antidotes to the pains of withdrawal and loneliness. If you live in a city and it is difficult to hike or go to the beach, then go to the nearest park or an area that is quiet. Sit with the trees and shrubs and just listen to all the things nature brings—the birds, crickets, leaves moving in the wind—and then listen to yourself. Pay attention to what the stillness brings in you. If you are in pain, sit with it for a while and then try to notice what aspects of your surroundings bring you pleasure and then sit with them. I recommend convening with nature as a part of your healing ritual. Do whatever it takes to bring reflective time spent outside into your life, even if it's only for short moments on those days when you have a bit of time to yourself. You'll be amazed at the results.

HELPING OTHERS

Helping others is another great way to get out of your head. Volunteer, be a mentor or big sister to an LGBTQ youth, or help at your local community center. Many twelve-step programs recommend working with other addicts who suffer with serious addiction as a way to diminish self-obsessive tendencies you may be struggling with. Getting sober from love addiction can be very consuming. Withdrawal can ignite obsessive thoughts that are hard to turn off. When you have had too much of yourself, reach out and help someone else. It will help you to stop thinking of yourself and your qualifier for a while, and you will most likely feel refreshed by the reprieve. Turning our attention to our friends and loved ones reminds us that those parts of our brain that are wired to connect are part of our survival. They encourage us to nurture our social network, which releases the feel-good chemicals we're longing for, but in a healthy way.

HOW TO SOOTHE YOURSELF

All of these are strategies designed to help you learn to self-soothe. Knowing that you can soothe yourself during times of stress—instead of reaching out to your ex, intriguing with that friend from work, or heading to the bar to meet someone new—will slowly build your confidence back. As you struggle to let go of urges, knowing that you can rely on yourself will help you regain trust in your ability to succeed at recovery—and in your life. One of the key ways to develop a solid relationship with yourself is to learn how to trust yourself. To do this, you must spend time alone. When you learn how to enjoy being alone (if this has been hard for you), it reminds you that you can take care of yourself no matter what arises.

Many of us who suffer from lesbian love addiction do not go into adulthood with an innate sense of self-trust. Some of us actually have the complete opposite. Self-trust was taken away during those difficult childhood and adolescent years. You'll begin to trust yourself more as you learn how to soothe yourself when you are anxious or triggered. However, if you are currently going through withdrawal, I would encourage you to reach out to everyone you know who is trustworthy and is equipped to help you get through this particular stage of healing. But once you are through the worst of your withdrawal, your next plan should be to try some of the soothing techniques: journaling, being in nature, going to therapy and meetings, finding a spiritual program that is the right fit for you, and, finally, befriending and understanding your inner critic.

MINDFULNESS AND MEDITATION

The benefits of mindfulness on our brain have been extensively studied since the 1970s. These studies show that meditation is one of the most effective ways to calm the mind, develop self-compassion, and understand who you really are.

In the 1970s Jon Kabat-Zinn founded the Stress Reduction Clinic at the University of Massachusetts Medical School to collect data on how mindfulness affected the brain. He has published many works on the subject, but one book that is particularly helpful is called *Mindfulness for Beginners: Reclaiming the Present Moment—and Your Life*. He defines mindfulness this way:

> Mindfulness is awareness, cultivated by paying attention in a sustained and particular way: on purpose, in the present moment, and non-judgmentally . . . in which we engage in (1) systematically regulating our attention and energy (2) thereby influencing and possibly

transforming the quality of our experiences (3) in the service of realizing the full range of our humanity and of (4) our relationship to others and the world. [19]

Benefits have been cited to include these healthy changes to the brain itself:

- Recognize, slow down, and stop automatic and habitual reactions.
- Respond more effectively to complex or difficult situations.
- See situations more clearly.
- Tap into your creative side.
- Achieve balance and resilience at work and at home. [20]

You can see how much this will help you heal your addicted brain. In our busy lives, it is not always easy to find time for meditation, but evidence shows how beneficial it is to our hearts and minds and to healing all the woes that befall us. I think your experience of it, should you try, will as well.

Combining a number of the different healing techniques above is the most effective way. For instance, imagine if you do some trauma healing work—release the trauma of your ex (and childhood issues) from your ANS and then practice mindfulness. What a powerful combination—healing paired with learning how to stay present. Whatever modalities you are drawn to, there is no greater gift you can give yourself than the opportunity to transform and evolve. Go ahead, you deserve it.

HOW TO HAVE A HEALTHY RELATIONSHIP WITH YOURSELF AND OTHERS

Healthy Boundaries

Most of us who suffer from lesbian love addiction did not grow up with healthy boundaries. Many of us grew up in homes in which addiction was present. Some of us may have even grown up with a parent whose overt or covert sex and love addiction undermined the health of the family. It's not uncommon for love addiction to exist and be out of everyone's awareness.

It's not surprising that so many lesbian love addicts have a hard time finding their voice, standing up for themselves, and saying no with confidence. Understandably, it is hard to do any of these things when you are afraid of rejection or abandonment and the idea of being vulnerable sounds too emotionally risky. Learning how to set healthy boundaries with yourself is an important start. Repeatedly saying yes to something you can't do because you don't want to upset someone is a sure way to slowly undermine your self-esteem. But as you get better at saying no when you mean no, you'll see that people are accepting of the new you. Setting and sticking to your bottom lines will help you trust yourself and find reward in being disciplined. A disciplined mind feels much better than an undisciplined one. Other healthy boundaries include engaging in your top-line behaviors even when you are stressed—such as exercise, meditation, journaling, and other types of inner work. Making sure you have fun is important too! Some addicts—once they get into recovery, can find themselves getting too serious—let yourself do the things that make you happy but are healthy and good for you.

Outer Boundaries

Lori Jean Glass from 5 Sister's Ranch developed a system in her program that teaches clients how to set inner and outer boundaries in their lives.[21] Outer boundaries are limits you set with another person that you disclose to them. For example, if one of your parents yells at you every time you visit, you can establish an outer boundary by explaining that you won't tolerate the behavior any more. You might say, "Stop, please. I am not going to stand here while you talk to me like this. I am leaving now," after which you walk away. If this is new behavior, the person you are setting this boundary with may not believe you at first. They probably won't take you too seriously, and they may continue to engage in the pattern in which the two of you are stuck in. You will probably have to set the boundary multiple times, but eventually they will get the message. Over time the person will see that you mean what you say, and that you are not engaging in this unhealthy behavior no matter how hard they try to pull you into the conflict. I am not saying this is easy, and you may have to practice setting your new boundaries before you implement them with any firmness. I advise working on this with your therapist and talking about it with your safe friends initially. You'll be amazed at how freeing this will become over time.

Inner Boundaries

According to Glass, inner boundaries are limits you establish with another person in your life that you are not required to disclose. In other words, you set them in your mind with your therapist, recovery partner, or friend. You do not need to discuss them with the person who triggered the need to set a boundary. Instead of explaining what they are or the reason for setting them, you simply adhere to them.

If you are having an issue with a loved one or friend, you may still be in a place where you wish they would change. This is also very normal. Most of us love people who we wish were different in certain ways, just like people who love us wish we were different in certain ways. When it comes to unhealthy or toxic conflict, wanting someone to change can seem like a survival technique. But the difficult truth is that you cannot bank on those around you changing for your life to get better. People will only change when they are ready and willing, just like you had to wait unti you were ready to face your love addiction. So since you cannot change someone who may treat you badly or is toxic in certain ways but you can't realistically get away from them, then safety planning and setting healthy outer boundaries is your most pragmatic solution. Other ways to deal with an unhealthy person is to limit your contact and time with them. Call a recovery partner or friend before and after you have to see this person. Prepare for your meetings so you can leave at a moment's notice if you have to. Don't set it up so that you end up stuck with someone who you know is going to yell, scream, shame, or blame you for something.

TOXIC PEOPLE

Then there are those people in your life who are so toxic that it is not advisable to continue a relationship with them. This could be a friend or family member whom you may have to cut out of your life to preserve and protect your emotional well-being. This may be a difficult decision to make, and an even harder one to carry out. You may need some time before you feel you are ready to do it, but if this person is not healthy for you, has no desire to change or grow, and you find this relationship is causing you nothing but pain, it is time to consider cutting it off, at least for an extended period. This decision should not be taken lightly, but sometimes it is the only way to achieve the peace of mind you deserve. How you decide to handle it is something to be further discussed with your therapist, recovery partners, or friends. Some women choose to write a letter explaining their need for a cutoff while asking the person to respect this newly set boundary.

DEVELOPING HEALTHY INTIMACY

Now for great news. Many of you have worked really hard to get to this place. You are finally ready to date in a healthy way. Congratulations! That is a huge accomplishment. The following is a short guide on "sober dating."[22]

Dating in Recovery

Mary came in to therapy really excited one day. She had met a woman she was attracted to. She had been sober from her love addiction for a year, and while she had not been looking for anyone, this woman appeared and the attraction was mutual. While she was cautiously optimistic, Mary wanted to be certain that she was practicing healthy dating and would hold on to her sense of self this time. After all, she'd done so much work to get here. She also wanted to make sure she wasn't attracted to anymore Janes or Tinas. She knew her past choices had been detrimental, and she wanted to guard her recovery. But there were also things she wanted from life—ongoing self-care, a healthy sustainable relationship, a fulfilling career, friends, family, and the activities she loved like traveling and being creative. She couldn't believe how much better her life had gotten since getting sober from her love addiction. In Mary's words:

> I had no idea this is what it would be like on the other side. No one could have told me this, of course. I had to go through everything I

did to get here but it is wonderful to feel free of that wretched addiction. I am no longer a slave to intriguing, inauthentic attention from women or fantasizing about the next actress in a movie I love.

She wanted to make sure that while dating she could stay present and not jump into the future like she had in the past, marrying the woman after two or three dates. "I want to take my time. I have no desire to merge. That in and of itself feels amazing," she told me.

This is called sober dating in SLAA terms.[23] Sober dating is another bottom-line tool we use when we return to the dating world. With the help of a sponsor, therapist, or recovery partner, people in love addiction recovery create a blueprint, an individually tailored sober dating plan that helps them stay away from behaviors that were harmful and that led to addictive behavior in the past.

A sober dating plan can look like this:

- Start with a phone call, then a coffee date, then a dinner date
- Maximum two dates a week for the first ninety days
- No physical contact beyond kissing for the first thirty days
- No sex of any kind before thirty days
- Minimal texting between dates, only to discuss logistics
- No texting of emotional material
- Avoid e-mailing as a way to communicate for the first thirty to sixty days
- Maximum of two emotionally based phone calls a week after thirty days of dating
- Keep core ways of connecting and relating to in-person encounters for the first ninety days
- Take at least one weekend trip before discussing any sort of future commitment
- Look for red flags

If dating turns into a relationship:

- No discussion of a future together for at least six months
- Stay connected to recovery buddies, sponsor, and friends while in the relationship
- Go to meetings, therapy, journal, and talk to safe friends about the relationship

- Don't keep secrets about your new girlfriend from safe friends or recovery partners
- Don't reveal everything to your new girlfriend right away
- Take your time to get to know your girlfriend
- Continue to watch for red flags

With the help of her closest recovery partners and several articles she had read in SLAA literature, Mary created a solid, sober dating plan that built her confidence. While these plans seemed a little harsh at first, Mary knew she needed them to serve as a guide through uncharted territory. She had never dated this consciously before, and she wanted to be appropriately cautious. She knew she was a merger, attracted to love avoidants, and addicted to the high of falling in love. This plan would help her stay grounded and balanced in her life.

If you follow these simple yet effective guidelines as you ease back into the dating world again, you will find that dating is an easier experience than ever before. Your anxiety about the outcome, your desperation to find someone as soon as possible, and your uneasiness around leading other women on—none of this will take over your decision-making process. You can return to the dating world recoverd from your love addiction and better able to develop healthy relationship with yourself and others. While attaching to a new person, once the honeymoon period is over, can be challenging (when both of your less than charming parts start to arise), you can feel confident you won't lose your sense of self in a relationship ever again. Remember, forming a new relationship is a process. Take your time—breathe into it—there is no rush. Now that you know that no woman or relationship is perfect, you can relax. The high will eventually shift and change, but with recovery and help from your sacred circle you know that you can navigate anything, and you are no longer addicted to the high of falling in love. Because of these changes inside of you, you will feel a new sense of liberation and freedom you did not know was possible. Now your life is your own. Your authentic self will guide you and help you stay grounded, real, and engaged in your life. Welcome!

NOTES

INTRODUCTION

1. UNC Charlotte, "Hetercentrism, Heterosexism, Homophobia," *Safe Zone*, accessed April 1, 2015, http://safezone.uncc.edu/lies/oppression#Heterocentrism,%20Heterosexism,%20Homophobia.

2. Joseph Gordon-Levitt, *Don Jon*, 2013; Steve McQueen, *Shame* (Beverly Hills, CA: 20th Century Fox Home Entertainment, 2012); Stuart Blumberg, *Thanks for Sharing*, 2014.

3. Blumberg et al., *Thanks for Sharing*.

4. Robert Weiss, *Cruise Control: Understanding Sex Addiction in Gay Men* (Los Angeles: Alyson Books, 2005).

5. Pia Mellody, Andrea Wells Miller, and Keith Miller, *Facing Love Addiction: Giving Yourself the Power to Change the Way You Love: The Love Connection to Codependence* (New York: HarperSan Francisco, 1992).

6. Ayisigi Hale Gonel, "Pansexual Identification in Online Communities: Employing a Collaborative Queer Method to Study Pansexuality," *Graduate Journal of Social Science* 10, no. 1 (February 2013): 36–59, http://search.ebscohost.com/login.aspx?direct=true&db=sih&AN=89513102&site=ehost-live.

7. Anne Wilson Schaef, *Escape from Intimacy: The Pseudo-Relationship Addictions: Untangling the "Love" Addictions, Sex, Romance, Relationships* (New York: Harper & Row, 1989); Mellody, Miller, and Miller, *Facing Love Addiction: Giving Yourself the Power to Change the Way You Love: The Love Connection to Codependence*; "S.L.A.A. Los Angeles," *S.L.A.A. Los Angeles*, accessed April 18, 2015, http://slaalosangeles.org/.

8. Mellody, Miller, and Miller, *Facing Love Addiction*.

9. Amir Levine and Rachel Heller, *Attached: The New Science of Adult Attachment and How It Can Help You Find — and Keep — Love* (New York: Jeremy P. Tarcher, 2010).

10. Mary D. Salter Ainsworth, *Patterns of Attachment: A Psychological Study of the Strange Situation* (Hillsdale, NJ: Lawrence Erlbaum Associates, 1978); John Bowlby, *Attachment and Loss* (New York: Basic Books, 1969).

11. Louann Brizendine, *The Female Brain* (New York: Morgan Road Books, 2006).

12. Levine and Heller, *Attached*.

13. Jennifer Young, *Loving Annabelle* (New Almaden, CA: Wolfe Video, 2006); Lisa Cholodenko, *High Art* (Universal City, CA: Universal, Focus Features, 2004); Pawel Pawlikowski, *My Summer of Love* (Universal City, CA: Universal Pictures, 2005); Sally Head et al., *Tipping the Velvet* (Silver Spring, MD: Distributed by Acorn Media, 2004); Ilene Chaiken, *The L Word: The Complete Series (Seasons 1–6)* (Hollywood, CA: Paramount Pictures, 2011); Ilene Chaiken, *The Real L Word. Season One* (Showtime Entertainment, Paramount Home Entertainment, 2010).

I. THE POWER OF OUR PHYSIOLOGY

1. "A Quote by Leah Raeder," Goodreads.com, accessed April 21, 2015, https://www.goodreads.com/quotes/6613231-girls-love-each-other-like-animals-there-is-something-ferocious.

2. Sue Johnson, *Hold Me Tight: Your Guide to the Most Successful Approach to Building Loving Relationships* (London: Piatkus, 2011).

3. Louann Brizendine, *The Female Brain* (New York: Morgan Road Books, 2006).

4. Cordelia Fine's book *Delusions: How Our Minds, Society and Neurosexism Creates Difference* critiques Brizendine's findings, calling it pseudo-science. Her work is worth exploring. I believe the truth lies somewhere in between each of these women's studies.

5. Norman Doidge, *The Brain That Changes Itself: Stories of Personal Triumph from the Frontiers of Brain Science* (New York: Viking, 2007).

6. Cordelia Fine, *Delusions of Gender: How Our Minds, Society, and Neurosexism Create Difference* (New York: W. W. Norton, 2011).

7. Susan Donaldson and James More, "One-Quarter of Gay Families Raising Kids," *ABC News*, June 23, 2011, http://abcnews.go.com/Health/sex-couples-census-data-trickles-quarter-raising-children/story?id=13850332.

8. Doidge, *The Brain That Changes Itself*, 94.

9. Rhawn Joseph, *Limbic System: Amygdala, Hypothalamus, Septal Nuclei, Cingulate, Hippocampus: Emotion, Memory, Language, Development, Evolution, Love, Attachment, Sexuality, Violence, Fear, Aggression, Amnesia, Dreams, Hallucinations, Abnormal Behavior* (Cambridge, MA: Cosmology Science Publishers, 2012).

10. Leslie Gartner, *The Autonomic Nervous System Made Ludicrously Simple* (Reisterstown, MA: Jen House Publishing Company, 2011).

11. Brizendine, *The Female Brain*.

12. Sarah Marshall, "Testosterone for Women," WebMD.com, April 14, 2012, http://www.webmd.com/women/testosterone-for-women.

13. Loretta Graziano Breuning, *Meet Your Happy Chemicals: Dopamine, Endorphin, Oxytocin, Serotonin* (Oakland, CA: System Integrity Press, 2012).

14. Bethany Brookshire, "Dopamine Is _____," Slate.com, July 3, 2013,http://www.slate.com/articles/health_and_science/science/2013/07/what_is_dopamine_love_lust_sex_addiction_gambling_motivation_reward.html.

2. THE WAY WE CONNECT

1. Eleanor Roosevelt, Lorena A. Hickok, and Rodger Streitmatter, *Empty without You: The Intimate Letters of Eleanor Roosevelt and Lorena Hickok* (Cambridge, MA: Da Capo Press, 2000), 16.

2. "Still Face Experiment: Dr. Edward Tronick," 2009, https://www.youtube.com/watch?v=apzXGEbZht0&feature=youtube_gdata_player.

3. Nancy Chodorow, *The Reproduction of Mothering: Psychoanalysis and the Sociology of Gender* (Berkeley: University of California Press, 1978).

4. Patricia Tjaden and Nancy Thoennes, *Full Report of the Prevalence, Incidence, and Consequences of Violence against Women: Findings from the National Violence against Women Survey*, Research Report (Washington, DC, and Atlanta, GA: U.S. Department of Justice, National Institute of Justice, and U.S. Department of Health and Human Services, Centers for Disease Control and Prevention, November 2000), http://www.nij.gov/topics/crime/intimate-partner-violence/pages/welcome.aspx.

5. Judith Bradford, Caitlin Ryan, and Esther D. Rothblum, "National Lesbian Health Care Survey: Implications for Mental Health Care," *Journal of Consulting and Clinical Psychology* 62, no. 2 (1994): 228.

6. Louann Brizendine, *The Female Brain* (New York: Morgan Road Books, 2006), 37.

7. "Secure, Insecure, Avoidant and Ambivalent Attachment in Mothers and Babies," 2011, https://www.youtube.com/watch?v=DH1m_ZMO7GU&feature=youtube_gdata_player.

8. Rick Nauert, "Brain Wiring Continues into Young Adulthood," Psych Central.com, accessed March 14, 2015, http://psychcentral.com/news/2011/09/23/brain-wiring-continues-into-young-adulthood/29719.html.

9. Amir Levine and Rachel Heller, *Attached: The New Science of Adult Attachment and How It Can Help You Find—and Keep—Love* (New York: Jeremy P. Tarcher, 2010).

10. Levine and Heller, *Attached*.

11. "What Is Your Attachment Style?" *Attachment Styles and Close Relationships*, accessed April 18, 2015, http://www.web-research-design.net/cgi-bin/crq/crq.pl.

3. WHAT IS UNIQUE ABOUT LESBIAN LOVE ADDICTION?

1. "Mary Gauthier, '"When a Woman Goes Cold' Lyrics; MetroLyrics," accessed April 21, 2015, http://www.metrolyrics.com/when-a-woman-goes-cold-lyrics-mary-gauthier.html.

2. Mark Z. Barabak, "Gays May Have the Fastest of All Civil Rights Movements," *Los Angeles Times*, May 20, 2012, http://articles.latimes.com/2012/may/20/nation/la-na-gay rights-movement-20120521.

3. "Indiana General Assembly, 2015 Session," accessed April 19, 2015, https://iga.in.gov/legislative/2015/bills/senate/568.

4. Kathleen Ritter and Anthony I. Terndrup, *Handbook of Affirmative Psychotherapy with Lesbians and Gay Men* (New York: Guilford Press, 2002).

5. Liz Margolies, Martha Becker, and Karla Jackson-Brewer, "Internalized Homophobia: Identifying and Treating the Oppressor Within," in *Lesbian Psychologies: Explorations and Challenges*, ed. Boston Lesbian Psychologies Collective (Urbana: University of Illinois Press, 1987), 229–41.

6. ADD INFORMATION.

7. Lee Zevy and Sahli A. Cavallaro, "Invisibility, Fantasy and Intimacy: Princess Charming Is Not a Prince," in *Lesbian Psychologies Explorations and Challenges*, ed. Boston Lesbian Psychologies Collective (Urbana: University of Illinois Press, 1987), 83–94, http://books.google.com/books?id=fiiGAAAAIAAJ.

8. Ritter and Terndrup, *Handbook of Affirmative Psychotherapy with Lesbians and Gay Men*.

9. UNC Charlotte, "Heterocentrism, Heterosexism, Homophobia," Safe Zone, accessed April 1, 2015, http://safezone.uncc.edu/allies/oppression#Heterocentrism,%20Heterosexism,%20Homophobia.

10. Adrienne Rich, *Compulsory Heterosexuality and Lesbian Existence* (London: Onlywomen Press, 1981).

11. Alan K. Malyon, "Psychotherpeutic Implications of Internalized Homophobia in Gay Men," in *Homosexuality and Psychotherapy: A Practitioner's Handbook of Affirmative Models*, ed. John C. Gonsiorek, vol. 4, *Research on Homosexuality* (New York: Haworth Press, 1982), 59–70.

12. Alan Blum and Von Pfetzing, "Assaults to the Self: The Trauma of Growing up Gay," *Gender and Psychoanalysis* 2, no. 4 (1997): 427–42.

13. Alan Carr, *Family Therapy: Concepts, Process, and Practice*, 2nd ed. (Chichester: Wiley, 2006).

14. William Shakespeare, *Hamlet* (New York: Pocket Books, 1958).

15. Lauren Costine, "Lesbianphobia" (Lesbian Identity, Antioch University Los Angeles, 2009).

16. Liz Margolies, Martha Becker, and Karla Jackson-Brewer, "Internalized Homophobia: Identifying and Treating the Oppressor Within," in *Lesbian Psychologies: Explorations and Challenges*, ed. Boston Lesbian Psychologies Collective (Urbana: University of Illinois Press, 1987), 229–41.

17. John Bradshaw, *Healing the Shame That Binds You* (Deerfield Beach, FL: Health Communications, 1988).

18. Lauren Lazin, *L Word Mississippi: Hate and Sin*, Documentary (Showtime, 2014), http://www.sho.com/sho/video/movies#.

19. Norman Doidge, *The Brain That Changes Itself: Stories of Personal Triumph from the Frontiers of Brain Science* (New York: Viking, 2007).

20. Emma Lazarus, Brainy Quotes. *Emma Lazarus Quotes*, http://www.brainyquote.com/quotes/authors/e/emma_lazarus.html, June 29, 2015.

21. Margolies, Becker, and Jackson-Brewer, "Internalized Homophobia."

22. Genevieve Weber-Gilmore, Sage Rose, and Rebecca Rubinstein, "The Impact of Internalized Homophobia on Outness for Lesbian, Gay, and Bisexual Individuals," *The Professional Counselor: Research and Practice* 1, no. 3 (April 2011): 163–75.

23. Ian Rivers and Anthony R. D'Augelli, "The Victimization of Lesbian, Gay, and Bisexual Youths," in *Lesbian, Gay, and Bisexual Identities and Youth: Psychological Perspectives*, ed. Anthony R. D'Augelli and Charlotte J. Patterson (New York: Oxford University Press, 2001), 199–223.

24. Doidge, *The Brain That Changes Itself*.

25. Gregory M. Herek, "Why Tell If You're Not Asked? Self-Disclosure, Intergroup Contact, and Heterosexuals' Attitudes toward Lesbians and Gay Men," in *Out in Force: Sexual Orientation and the Military*, ed. Gregory M.

Herek, Jared B. Jobe, and Ralph M. Carney (Chicago: University of Chicago Press, 1996).

26. Bonnie Weiss, *Illustrated Workbook for Self-Therapy for Your Inner Critic: Transforming Self-Criticism into Self-Confidence* (Larkspur, CA: Pattern System Books, 2011).

27. Karyl McBride, *Will I Ever Be Good Enough?: Healing the Daughters of Narcissistic Mothers* (New York: Free Press, 2008).

28. Karen Reivich and Andrew Shatte, *The Resilience Factor: 7 Keys to Finding Your Inner Strength and Overcoming Life's Hurdles* (New York: Broadway Books, 2003).

29. *Princely Goddess Inanna Initiates Her Devoted Priestess Bride: How Ancient Lesbian Wisdom Traditions Can Inspire a New Vulvically Vivifying Lesbian-Centered Myth of Meaning for All Women*, vol. 1, 5 vols., Singing the Heavenly Muse of Lesbian Individuation for All Women: Introductory Series on the Theory and Practice of Sapphic Psychoanalysis, 2012, https://www.youtube.com/watch?v=AQ7jMFVZZG0&feature=youtube_gdata_player.

30. Neil Miller, *Out of the Past: Gay and Lesbian History from 1869 to the Present* (New York: Vintage Books, 1995).

31. Olivia M. Espin, "Issues of Identity in the Psychology of Latina Lesbians," in *Lesbian Psychologies: Explorations and Challenges*, ed. Boston Lesbian Psychologies Collective (Urbana: University of Illinois Press, 1987), 35–55.

32. Brian Lowry, "Risks and Benefits Seen for an Out-of-the-Closet 'Ellen,'" *Los Angeles Times*, March 3, 1997, http://articles.latimes.com/1997-03-03/entertainment/ca-34276_1_ellen-morgan.

33. Tonda L. Hughes and Sharon C. Wilsnack, "Use of Alcohol among Lesbians: Research and Clinical Implications," *American Journal of Orthopsychiatry* 67, no. 1 (1997): 20–36.

4. HOW WE MERGE AND SPIRAL

1. Audre Lorde, "'Recreation Poem' by Audre Lorde—Poem Hunter," PoemHunter.com, accessed April 19, 2015, http://www.poemhunter.com/poem/recreation-6/?utm_source=facebook&utm_campaign=tavsiye_et.

2. American Psychiatric Association and DSM-5 Task Force, *Diagnostic and Statistical Manual of Mental Disorders: DSM-5* (Washington, DC: American Psychiatric Association, 2013).

3. "Substance Abuse and Emotion," accessed April 19, 2015, http://www.apa.org/pubs/books/4318059.aspx.

4. "Public Policy Statement: Definition of Addiction," American Society of Addiction Medicine, August 15, 2011, http://www.asam.org/docs/publicy-policy-statements/1definition_of_addiction_long_4-11.pdf?sfvrsn=2.

5. "What Is a Process Addiction? (with Pictures)," wiseGEEK.org, accessed April 19, 2015, http://www.wisegeek.org/what-is-a-process-addiction.htm.

6. Helen E. Fisher et al., "Reward, Addiction, and Emotion Regulation Systems Associated with Rejection in Love," *Journal of Neurophysiology* 104, no. 1 (2010): 51.

7. Pia Mellody, Andrea Wells Miller, and Keith Miller, *Facing Love Addiction: Giving Yourself the Power to Change the Way You Love: The Love Connection to Codependence* (New York: HarperSan Francisco, 1992).

8. Lori Jean Glass, "Love Addiction and Codependent Relationship Treatment," accessed April 19, 2015, http://www.fivesistersranch.com/.

9. Carl R. Rogers, *On Becoming a Person: A Therapist's View of Psychotherapy* (Boston: Houghton Mifflin, 1961).

10. Patrick Carnes, *The Betrayal Bond: Breaking Free of Exploitive Relationships* (Deerfield Beach, FL: Health Communications, 1997), 15.

11. Mellody, Miller, and Miller, *Facing Love Addiction*.

12. Emily Troscianko, "Recovering from Anorexia: How and Why to Start," *Psychology Today*, accessed April 19, 2015, http://www.psychologytoday.com/blog/hunger-artist/201501/recovering-anorexia-how-and-why-start.

13. The Asexual Visibility and Education Network (AVEN), *An Asexual Is a Person Who Does Not Experience Sexual Attraction*. Retrieved on April 11, 2015, from http://www.asexuality.org/home/.

14. Philip Blumstein and Pepper Schwartz, *American Couples: Money, Work, Sex* (New York: Morrow, 1983).

15. Suzana Rose, *Lesbian Violence Fact Sheet*. National Violence against Women Prevention Research Center, University of Missouri at St. Louis, accessed April 19, 2015, https://mainweb-v.musc.edu/vawprevention/lesbianrx/factsheet.shtml.

16. Rose, *Lesbian Violence Fact Sheet*; Gwat-Yong Lie and Sabrina Gentlewarrier, "Intimate Violence in Lesbian Relationships," *Journal of Social Service Research* 15, no. 1–2 (November 19, 1991): 41–59, doi:10.1300/J079v15n01_03.

5. WITHDRAWAL

1. Emily Dickinson, "The Complete Poems of Emily Dickinson," Bartleby.com, 1924, www.bartleby.com/113/.

2. Margaret Reynolds and Sappho, *The Sappho Companion* (New York: Palgrave, 2002), 43.

3. Eric Metcalf, MPH, "Can You Die of a Broken Heart? Broken Heart Syndrome May Often Be Confused with Symptoms of a Heart Attack," WebMD, accessed April 20, 2015, http://www.webmd.com/heart/features/broken-heart-syndrome-stress-cardiomyopathy.

4. Ibid.

5. Elaine Hatfield and Susan Sprecher, "Measuring Passionate Love in Intimate Relationships," *Journal of Adolescence* 9, no. 4 (1986): 383–410.

6. Doodlekit Free Website Builder, "Withdrawal," *E Sober Buddy*, accessed April 20, 2015, http://www.esoberbuddy.com/home/withdrawal.

7. "Opiate Withdrawal: MedlinePlus Medical Encyclopedia," accessed April 20, 2015, http://www.nlm.nih.gov/medlineplus/ency/article/000949.htm.

8. *Sex and Love Addicts Anonymous* (Boston: Augustine Fellowship, Sex and Love Addicts Anonymous, Fellowship-Wide Services, 1986).

9. *Sex and Love Addicts Anonymous.*

10. Natalie Lue, *The No Contact Rule—Natalie Lue* (Caterham, England: Naughty Girl Media, 2013).

11. Ilene Chaiken et al., *The L Word. The Complete Series (Seasons 1–6)* (Hollywood, CA: Paramount Pictures, 2011).

12. Valieriya Safronova, "Exes Explain Ghosting, the Ultimate Silent Treatment," *New York Times*, June 26, 2015, http://www.nytimes.com/2015/06/26/fashion/exes-explain-ghosting-the-ultimate-silent-treatment.html?_r=0.

13. Craig Nakken, *The Addictive Personality: Understanding the Addictive Process and Compulsive Behavior* (Center City, MN: Hazelden, 1996).

14. David Bissette, "Your Bottom Line," Healthymind.com, 2004, http://healthymind.com/bottom-line.pdf.

15. *Alcoholics Anonymous: The Story of How Many Thousands of Men and Women Have Recovered from Alcoholism* (New York: Alcoholics Anonymous World Services, 2001).

16. Doodlekit Free Website Builder, "Withdrawal."

17. Gerald A. Juhnke and W. Bryce Hagedorn, *Counseling Addicted Families: An Integrated Assessment and Treatment Model* (New York: Routledge, 2006).

18. Fisher et al., "Reward, Addiction, and Emotion Regulation Systems," 57.

19. Elisabeth Kubler-Ross, "Elisabeth Kubler-Ross—Five Stages of Grief," trans. Alan Chapman, Businessballs.com, 2006, http://www.businessballs.com/elisabeth_kubler_ross_five_stages_of_grief.htm#elisabeth_kubler-ross_five_stages_of_grief.

20. Kelly McDaniel, *Ready to Heal: Breaking Free of Addictive Relationships* (Carefree, AZ: Gentle Path Press, 2012).

6. HOW TO HAVE A HEALTHY RELATIONSHIP WITH YOURSELF AND OTHERS

1. "30 Mind-Bending Carl Jung Quotes—The Unbounded Spirit," accessed April 21, 2015, http://theunboundedspirit.com/30-mind-bending-carl-jung-quotes/.

2. *Sex and Love Addicts Anonymous* (Boston: Augustine Fellowship, Sex and Love Addicts Anonymous, Fellowship-Wide Services, 1986).

3. Brenée Brown, *I Thought It Was Just Me (But It Isn't): Making the Journey from "What Will People Think?" to "I Am Enough"* (New York: Gotham Books, 2008).

4. Joseph Campbell and Joseph Campbell Foundation, *The Hero with a Thousand Faces* (Novato, CA: New World Library, 2008).

5. Andy Wachowski and Lana Wachowski, *The Matrix* (Burbank, CA: Warner Bros. Pictures: Distributed by Warner Home Video, 2001).

6. Bonnie Weiss, *Illustrated Workbook for Self-Therapy for Your Inner Critic: Transforming Self-Criticism into Self-Confidence* (Larkspur, CA: Pattern System Books, 2011).

7. Weiss, *Illustrated Workbook for Self-Therapy*.

8. Elaine Miller-Karas, *Building Resilience to Trauma: The Trauma and Community Resilience Models* (New York: Routledge, 2015).

9. Francine Shapiro, *Eye Movement Desensitization and Reprocessing Therapies*, The EMDR Institute, 1990, http://www.emdr.com/.

10. Bstan-'dzin-rgya-mtsho, Dalai Lama XIV, and Howard C. Cutler, *The Art of Happiness: A Handbook for Living* (New York: Riverhead Books, 2009).

11. Pema Chodromy, *Getting Unstuck: Breaking Your Habitual Patterns and Encountering Naked Reality* (Boulder, CO: Sounds True, 2005).

12. Brené Brown, *Daring Greatly: How the Courage to Be Vulnerable Transforms the Way We Live, Love, Parent, and Lead* (New York: Gotham Books, 2012).

13. Jeremiah Abrams and Connie Zweig, *Meeting the Shadow: The Hidden Power of the Dark Side of Human Nature* (Los Angeles: J. P. Tarcher, 1991).

14. Ban Bossy is a new online movement that is challenging the way girls are viewed and educated. Please check out their website and download their Ban Bossy Leadership Tips for Girls. I recommend these lessons for the little girl in you who was taught maladaptive coping mechanisms like saying sorry for every

little thing, not speaking up in class, and being taught to let the boys dominate. They have some great tips for women at any age.

15. "Ban Bossy: Encourage Girls to Lead," accessed April 21, 2015, http:// banbossy.com/.

16. *Sex and Love Addicts Anonymous.*

17. Linda C. Senn, *The Many Faces of Journaling: Topics and Techniques for Personal Journal Writing* (St. Louis, MO: Pen Central Press, 2001).

18. "Nature, the Greatest Teacher—News," accessed April 21, 2015, http:// communicate.eckharttolle.com/news/2013/12/11/nature-the-greatest-teacher/.

19. Jon Kabat-Zinn, *Mindfulness for Beginners: Reclaiming the Present Moment—And Your Life* (Boulder, CO: Sounds True, 2012), 1.

20. "What Is Mindfulness?" Mindfulnet.org, accessed April 20, 2015, http:// www.mindfulnet.org/page2.htm#Top5.

21. Lori Jean Glass, "Love Addiction and Codependent Relationship Treatment," accessed April 19, 2015, http://www.fivesistersranch.com/.

22. *Sex and Love Addicts Anonymous.*

23. *Sex and Love Addicts Anonymous.*

INDEX

abandonment: fear of, 65, 72–73; trauma bond as, 81

abstinent behaviors, 100–101, 102; as bottom line, 101; as middle line, 101; as top line, 101

ACC. *See* anterior cingulate cortex

acceptance, as grief stage 5, 109

acting out, 100

addiction: acting out in, 100; alcoholism as, xiv, xv, 31; books on, 62; criteria of, 60; drugs as, xiv, xv; identification of, 59–60; lesbian rates of, 57–58; love as, xiii–xiv, xv; as process addiction, 59–60; as seduction addiction, 70–71; self-hatred in, 58; sex as, xv; SLAA for, xvi, 84, 89–90; treatment of, xxvii; twelve-step program against, xv, 94–95, 126–127

addiction criteria: from American Psychiatric Association, 59–60; from ASAM, 59–60

adolescence: coming out in, 25; hormones during, 24, 43; lesbian vulnerability in, 24, 44; negative self-talk in, 43; oxytocin/dopamine rush in, 27; same-sex love in, 25

adulthood: attachment styles in, 32–33; coming out in, 25; finding a mate in, 31

Ainsworth, Mary, xx–xxi

alcohol addiction, xiv, xv, 31

alone intolerant, love addicts as, 69

American Couples (Schwartz and Blumstein), 85

American Psychiatric Association, 59–60

American Society of Addiction Medicine (ASAM), 59–67

amygdala, 6, 8

anger, as grief stage 2, 106

Anna, 69

anorexia, sexual, 83–85

ANS. *See* autonomic nervous system

anterior cingulate cortex (ACC), 7, 21

The Art of Happiness (Dalai Lama and Cutler), 122–123

ASAM. *See* American Society of Addiction Medicine

Attached: The New Science of Adult Attachment and How It Can Help You Find and Keep Love (Levine & Heller), xix, xxi, 32–33

attachment: Bowlby and Ainsworth on, xx–xxi; patterns of, xx–xxiv, 19–20; theory of, xxi–xxii, 28

attachment styles: as adult, 32–33; as anxious, 33, 34–35; as anxious-avoidant, 30; as anxious-resistant, 30; as avoidant, 35–36, 60–61; as disorganized, 30; as love addiction, 35–36, 60–61; as love avoidant, 35–36, 60–61; as secure, 29, 33

autonomic nervous system (ANS), 7, 8–9, 9; healing through, 112; as inside CNS,

7; qualifier triggering, 104–105; TRM
healing, 121–122

bargaining, as grief stage 3, 106–107
belief system damage, 50–51
*The Betrayal Bond: Breaking Free of
Exploitive Relationships* (Carnes), 81
bi-sexual, xvi
Bissette, David: abstinence bottom line
of, 100–101; abstinent behaviors of,
101, 102
Black Iris (Raeder), 1
Blumstein, Phillip, 85
books: on addiction, 62; inner-critic
workbooks as, 121; on sex addiction,
xvi, xix
bottom line behavior: abstinence as, 101;
from Bissette, 100–101; lacking in love
addiction, 64–65; money issues in, 100;
no contact as, 95–96; no dating as, 97;
no fantasizing as, 98–99; no porn/
masturbation as, 99–100; no seduction
as, 96–97; SLAA on, 94–95
bottom line worksheet, 102
boundaries: for relationship health,
132–134; against toxic people,
134–135. *See also* bottom line behavior
Bowlby, John, xx–xxi
brain physiology, 8; female/male
differences of, 5–6; of gay women, 3, 4;
in love addiction, 2–3, 7; pleasure
center in, 13–14; sexual plasticity of, 4;
structures of, 6–7, 7; in utero, 5–6, 17;
in withdrawal, 101–105
*The Brain That Changes Itself: Stories of
Personal Triumph from the Frontiers
of Brain Science* (Doidge), 4
breastfeeding, 12
Brizendine, Louann, 2–3, 4, 5, 6; on
female life cycle, 17, 36; on oxytocin/
dopamine rush, 27
broken heart, 90–91
Brown, Brene, 124
butch/boi, 4, 55; Charley as, 23; Tanya as,
33; Tina as, xviii

Campbell, Joseph, 116–118
Carla, 51
Carmen, of *The L Word*, 68

Carnes, Patrick, xxvi, 81, 83
case study, of love addiction, xvii–xix, 31,
89–90
central nervous system (CNS): ANS
inside, 7; cortisol in, 11; healing
through, 112; serotonin in, 13; TRM
healing, 121–122; in withdrawal,
101–105
Charley, 23, 24, 61, 62, 85; alcohol
addiction of, 31; finding a mate, 31;
lacking bottom lines, 64–65; low self-
esteem of, 68; mother rejecting, 24; as
seeking real intimacy, 75–76; sexual
assault of, 26, 27–28; slip of, 111;
withdrawal bottom lines of, 96, 97,
99–100
child abuse, 82
Chodorow, Nancy, 21
Chodron, Pema, 123–124
Chuck, 56
CNS. *See* central nervous system
coming out, xiv; in adolescence, 25; in
adulthood, 25; love addiction in, 25
community recovery groups, 127–128
cortisol, 11
*Cruise Control: Understanding Sex
Addiction in Gay Men* (Weiss, R.), xxvi
Cutler, Howard, 122–123

Dalai Lama, 122–123
Danielle, 68, 69; Josie smothering, 75;
Josie with, 107, 108–109
*Daring Greatly: How the Courage to Be
Vulnerable Transforms the Way We
Live, Love, Parent and Lead* (Brown),
124
depression, as grief stage 4, 108–109
development stages: adolescence, 24, 25,
27; coming out in, 25; female
hormones in, 10–11; as fetal, 4, 5, 17,
18, 20; as girlhood, 21, 22; as infant,
18–19, 19, 19–20, 21, 29–30; of lesbian
identity, 51–52; mapping the self
through, 52–53; sexual assault within,
25
*Diagnostic and Statistical Manual of
Mental Disorders* 5e (DSM-5), 59, 91
Dickinson, Emily, 89